AMERICA
AND ITS INDIANS

By Dr. JEROME E. LEAVITT

Illustrated by ROBERT GLAUBKE

For thousands of years — and perhaps longer — Indians have lived on the North American continent. Here they hunted wild game and fowl, and fished in the streams and rivers. The so-called civilized part of the world knew nothing about them until Christopher Columbus "discovered" them, along with the New World. Thinking that he had sailed to India, Columbus bestowed upon the natives who greeted him the name "Indians."

Indians, at one time or another, lived in all parts of America. They were split up into many tribes, but their way of life was generally dependent on the terrain of the area in which they settled. In the desert regions, at the southern part of the Rocky Mountains, villages sprang up close to precious water sources. Here the living quarters at first were in caves along canyon walls, and later were built from stone or adobe, in structures called pueblos. On the great stretches of flat country, the Plains Indians hunted buffalo and sheltered themselves with driftwood houses covered with grass and roofed with earth. From the Mississippi River eastward, where vast forest lands prevailed, the Indians of this section built houses of poles covered with the bark of trees and fashioned canoes from hollowed-out tree trunks or from birch-bark.

Within the pages of this fascinating book, Dr. Jerome E. Leavitt both enlightens and entertains the reader by methodically reviewing all of the distinctive and exciting facets of the American Indian, from coast to coast. He sees the Indians as colorful people with varied cultures. He tells of their food, houses, clothes and crafts — not merely as matters of record, but as living history — touching as well on their customs, form of government, social life and religion. The span of coverage is from the Indians of antiquity to the Indians of today, resulting in a comprehensive picture of the red man in America.

Robert Glaubke contributes generously of his artistic talents with a full-page color illustration for each of 35 tribes — including, in turn, Indians of the Northwest, California, the Southwest, the Plains and the Eastern woodlands — plus many other supplementary pictures which are notable for their authenticity of likeness and feeling.

AMERICA AND ITS INDIANS

AMERICA AND ITS INDIANS

By DR. JEROME E. LEAVITT

Professor of Education, Portland State College, Portland, Oregon

Illustrations by ROBERT GLAUBKE

CHILDRENS PRESS · CHICAGO

Library of Congress Catalog Card Number: 62-9078
Copyright, 1962, Childrens Press
Printed in the U.S.A.

ACKNOWLEDGMENTS

The author wishes to express his appreciation and gratitude to all those who helped him in the preparation of this book.

Special acknowledgment is made for the help given by:

Dr. Harry T. Getty
Associate Professor, Department of Anthropology
University of Arizona, Tucson, Arizona

Dr. John Eliot Allen
Professor, Department of Geology
Portland State College, Portland, Oregon

Dr. Charles S. Brant
Associate Professor, Department of Anthropology
Portland State College, Portland, Oregon

Lillian I. Mosher
Elementary Supervisor, Portland Public Schools
Portland, Oregon

▲▲▲▲▲▲▲▲▲▲▲▲▲▲▲▲▲▲▲▲▲▲▲▲▲▲▲▲▲▲▲▲▲

CONTENTS

PREFACE

I have written "America and Its Indians" because I always have been interested in the American Indians and count as friends some of these people. I hope that you, too, will find them interesting, learn more about them and perhaps someday also have friends among them.

This book differs from many other books on Indians because it is concerned with details of the daily lives of Indians within certain tribes in North America rather than with Indians in general.

The book opens with the story of the Indians who were here thousands of years before the arrival of the white man and ends with a description of Indian life today. There is specific information on about thirty-six tribes, their environment, subsistence activities, houses, clothes and crafts. Also included, when of special interest, are a few interesting details of political organization, social structure and religious practice of certain tribes.

In order to group the Indian tribes so that their stories could be told most effectively, the continent has been divided into five cultural areas. These are: the Northwest Coast, the California region, the Southwest, the Plains, and the Eastern Woodlands. A separate chapter has been devoted to each of these.

JEROME E. LEAVITT
July, 1961

Chapter I

BEFORE THE WHITE MAN

Men had lived in America for over fifteen thousand years before Columbus made his discovery in 1492. At the time of the first contact with Europeans some of the people, later known as Indians, were hunters that roamed the land in search of game, others lived in simple villages and tended their crops, while still others lived in towns. These people spoke many different languages, had quite different political systems, and had many different religious beliefs.

The ancestors of these Indians had to discover America themselves before they could occupy it. Although we do not have absolute proof, many anthropologists believe that these Indians first came from Asia to America over a land bridge that once joined the two continents. There is some evidence that America was populated by these bands of wandering hunters who came from Asia by way of Alaska. If these people did make this trip over the land bridge their principal possessions were probably fire and chipped stone spear points, stone knives, and some sort of clothing.

It is believed that once these small bands of hunters crossed over what is now the Bering Strait into America, many of them wandered south following the game animals as they went. The men carried their spears, and the women strapped their babies to their backs. Dogs and children followed along as best they could. Thus, they wandered back and forth leaving only a few clues indicating where they went and what they did.

Actually America was discovered three times. The first discovery was by these Indians who came over the Bering Straits; the second was by Leif Ericson about 1,000 A.D. when he spent the winter

13

*Many anthropologists believe that small
wandering bands of hunters came to America
from Asia across a land bridge that joined the
continents at the point where Bering Strait
is now.*

below Cape Cod in Massachusetts; the third was the one that we are most familiar with, by Columbus.

It was Columbus who gave the Indians their name since he mistakenly thought he had landed in India. He did not know this continent existed. The term "red men" is not a true name either, as most of our native Americans have skin colors that range through various shades of brown.

Year after year more and more old stone tools and projectile points are being found that indicate that man has lived in the Americas a long time. Of particular importance are the Folsom points that have been found from Alberta and Saskatchewan, Canada, on the north to New Mexico in the south. They have been found as far east as New York.

Folsom is the name given to a particular type of fluted point because it was found near Folsom, New Mexico. This Folsom find is estimated to be about ten thousand years old. These finds indicate some degree of cultural relationship among the early people.

Many recently discovered caves also provide evidence of early occupation. These caves were found to have fifteen feet or more of debris left behind by their early occupants. These deposits are in layers which indicate that succeeding groups of people occupied these caves over a period of thousands of years.

Of all of the caves, the one in the Sandia Mountains east of Albuquerque, New Mexico, and Ventana Cave in the Castle Mountains of southern Arizona are the most important and interesting. Digging parties from the University of New Mexico working in the Sandia Cave found Folsom points under a layer of material that was probably left by Indians living there some time before Columbus. On digging below the second layer which contained the Folsom materials, still a third layer was found. In this third layer, points and animal bones were found that resembled those found in Asia.

When Ventana Cave was excavated by parties from the University of Arizona, they found fifteen feet of deposits left there by many

*Early Indian chipping
an arrowhead from flint*

groups of people over many thousands of years. The bottom layer of materials resembled the Folsom materials. Succeeding layers on up to the top showed evidence of succeeding cultures through those of the time of Columbus and up to fairly recent years.

It was at the end of the Ice Age that people began to drift into North America from Asia down the ice-free valleys into Alaska and Canada. These early people lived mainly on the animals that they hunted. These early immigrants are now known as Paleo-Indians. Some time after the migration of these Paleo-Indians many of the animals that they hunted, the mastadon, the sabre-toothed tiger, the giant bear, became extinct.

We have no knowledge about the clothing that Paleo-Indians wore, except sandals found in Oregon. This indicates that they did not always go barefoot. It is likely that they made garments, moccasins, and tents of animal skins. Bone needles and stone knives have been found among their tools. Scraping and rubbing stones that could have been used to clean hides have also been found in quantity. Stone and bone beads and pendants indicate that they did dress up and did create some art forms.

At this point you might begin to wonder how archeologists, the men who study objects left behind by past generations, know how old these objects are. These archeologists use a process called the Carbon 14 technique. This is based on determining the amount of radio-active Carbon 14 left in ancient materials, particularly in charcoal. Scientists also have ways of telling the age of stone and metal.

There has been increasing evidence that during the Paleo-Indian period, the people who lived on the eastern side of the Rocky Mountains and those who lived on the western side had different ways of life and produced different tools.

In the east the emphasis was on big game hunting and in the west, the gathering of plant products was the chief occupation.

After these early hunters had roamed over most of America, a new way of life was developed. Although still hunters they were less

16

As early hunters drifted down ice-free valleys, they hunted animals that are now extinct. The biggest of these was the mammoth which they drove into a pit and then killed with stones and spears.

roving, and had a higher standard of living. One of their principal achievements was in cooking. They boiled some of their food with hot stones. This was done by dropping large, hot pebbles in vessels of wood, bark, skin, or basketry that contained the food. When the pebbles cooled, in the food being cooked, they were returned to the fire to be reheated. These stones were handled with wooden tongs.

Cooking with hot stones was a step toward a higher standard of living

In time, these Indians, known to researchers as Stone-boilers, made some of the finest baskets known. Today many of these baskets can be seen in museums. Many baskets were woven tight enough to hold water. These people are often referred to as the Basket-makers rather than Stone-boilers.

During this period of time acorn meal came to be one of the staple foods. First the acorns were cracked. The meats were then dried and ground. Then hot water was poured through this meal a number of times to soak out the tannic acid that would make it bitter. The meal was mixed with water to make a dough which was either baked on a hot stone near a fire or made into a soup. Sometimes mint or other leaves were added to the acorn soup to give it a different flavor.

Stone-boilers that lived near streams, rivers, lakes, or the ocean often used fish in place of acorns.

Following the Indian culture known as the Stone-boilers or Basket-makers, from their way of life, was another culture or way of life in which both farming and pottery making were developed. This period of time is not nearly so long ago as the time of the roaming hunters or the more settled Stone-boilers.

We are so used to farming and gardening that it seems strange to us that early man did not know about it, too. Some people had to invent the various aspects of farming. Although the making of fire is considered to be the greatest discovery of all time, the development of agriculture is placed next in line in importance.

The early Indians probably began gardening by first protecting plants that were useful to them. Then sooner or later they started collecting seeds and planting them. These prehistoric Indians throughout North and South America planted and raised potatoes, tobacco, maize, tomatoes, chocolate, and a number of other useful plants.

Corn was one of the most important seed plants developed. It was probably brought up from Mexico where it had been grown for a long time. Beans were also brought to North America from Mexico.

19

The Navaho and Pueblo Indians of a later period depended on corn and beans. Many legends have been written about how the Indians first got corn.

It has not been possible to determine just where pottery was invented, for early pieces have been found in many places. One legend tells us that baskets used to be lined with clay and corn was heated in them. Then it was discovered that the clay lining could be lifted out and used as a container. Later, other people made various containers out of clay and hardened them by putting them in a fire to bake.

After our very early American Indians had a more secure source of food, and containers in which to hold and cook food, they had more time to improve the places in which they lived. Various kinds of shelters were built.

During this same period of time Indian groups in what is now Ohio and Illinois were spending their time building large mounds. These were huge earth structures sometimes as high as one-hundred feet. Thousands of these mounds have been discovered. Some of these mounds were used as burial places. Others functioned as religious edifices. Today, along with the skeletons in these mounds, great amounts of mica, pearls, and carved stone pipes have been discovered. Although they built large mounds, these people lived in crude cabins made of poles and bark.

A few hundred years before the coming of the white man the making of pipes became quite an art. They were carved out of many different kinds of materials. Many were decorated with feathers and various other ornamental materials. By the time white men arrived from Europe, the pipe was used in religious ceremonies. When a stranger came bearing a decorated pipe it was known that he came in a spirit of peace and friendship. You have probably heard the expression, "Smoking the pipe of peace." This meant that those who smoked one of these grand pipes became brothers and would live in peace and friendship.

After these prehistoric periods of time the Spanish came into North America by way of Mexico, followed by the French and English who first settled on the eastern coast and then started to move westward. As the number of pioneers, traders, travelers, and missionaries increased, reports were collected about many different Indian groups living in North America. These reports told of Indian tribes speaking many different languages, eating different kinds of food, living in different kinds of houses, and having different religious ceremonies.

As more and more information was collected, it was discovered that Indians living in a given area tended to have many things in common and those living in another area were likely to do things in quite a different way.

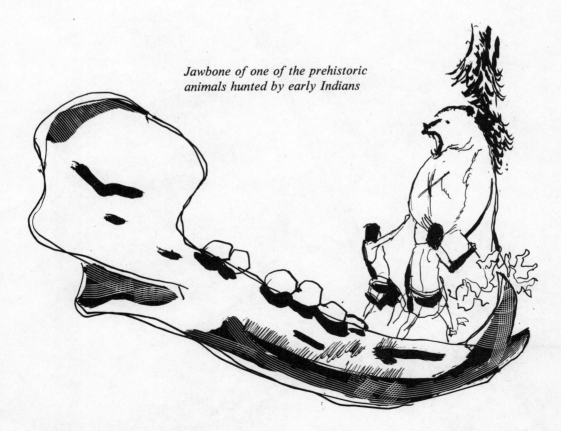

Jawbone of one of the prehistoric animals hunted by early Indians

*Typical artifacts of early
Indians of the Northwest*

Chapter II ▲ INDIANS OF
THE NORTHWEST COAST

THE INDIANS of the Northwest Coast occupied a narrow coastal strip now included in the states of Washington, Oregon, and the Canadian Coast area up into Alaska.

This part of the United States and Canada is known as the Pacific Mountain System. This system is made up of some low coastland, a coastal range of mountains, an interior valley, and the Cascade Mountains that separate this area from the inland plateau.

Due to the mountain ranges, the rainfall is heavy and produces abundant vegetation. The Japanese Current offshore keeps the climate moderate even in the higher latitudes. Most days are frost free. In the valleys the temperature is not extreme, either in summer or winter. The mountains abound with evergreens such as fir and spruce; and the valleys with pine, fir, and hemlock.

Indians in this region secured their food by hunting wild animals, gathering plant products, and catching fish. The major subsistence activity was concerned with the bounty of the sea. The sea and rivers provided a great amount and variety of foods such as fish, whales, porpoises, and sea otters.

Because such items as fish, berries, and edible plants are seasonal, periods of intense food preparation became necessary in order to preserve the food when it was available. In between the busy periods of food preparation, time was available for other activities. The presence of wood of a variety of types made possible the development of a number of crafts such as woodworking and weaving. In woodworking they made storage boxes, cradles, canoes, carved dishes, totem poles, and houses. They wove blankets and articles of clothing.

Prior to the time of Columbus this rich land of the Pacific Northwest served as a melting pot where tribes from the interior of America mixed with new arrivals from Asia. The Indians occupying this coastal area differed a great deal in language and physical characteristics even though they had many other things in common. Some of these spoke a language related to the Athapascan of the interior plateau. Others spoke languages related to Tsimshian, which was quite different.

The groups living in Canada and Northern Washington, in general, were tall, muscular and had light skin. Those on the Southern Washington and Oregon Coast tended to be shorter, broad chested, and somewhat darker in skin color than their northern neighbors.

At the present time archeologists have not unearthed enough evidence to indicate whether the Indians who greeted the early settlers were reasonably new comers or whether they had been in the area for thousands of years.

In 1741 a boat was sent ashore from a Russian ship to make contact with the Tlingit. The crew never returned and were presumed killed by them. A Spanish ship tied up at Nootka Sound and natives that came out were given silver spoons. However, the first important contact was made by Captain Cook when he stopped at Nootka Sound and traded for sea-otter skins.

It was not long before ships from England, Spain, Russia, and America were assigned to the Northwest Indian trade. At first the Indians traded furs for iron knives and adz blades. After the Indians had a sufficient quantity of these, the traders used trinkets such as beads and iron bracelets for barter. As these fads wore off traders had to provide guns, molasses, rice, and rum to trade for furs. Soon business increased and the traders began to trade skins, furs, and slaves from one tribe to another.

A number of land-based traders tried to set up trading posts only to have them destroyed by the Indians. The Russians were able to set up and hold one post in 1804 at Fort Archangel near

*Northwest Indians raising a
totem pole into position*

modern Sitka. When the Hudson Bay and Northwest Company joined forces in 1821 the way was opened for a series of trading posts that extended up and down the coast. The most famous of these being Fort Langley, Fort Simpson, and Fort McLoughlin.

A large number of Indian tribes occupied the Northwest Coastal area when white man first came. The descendents of some of these still live in the same place.

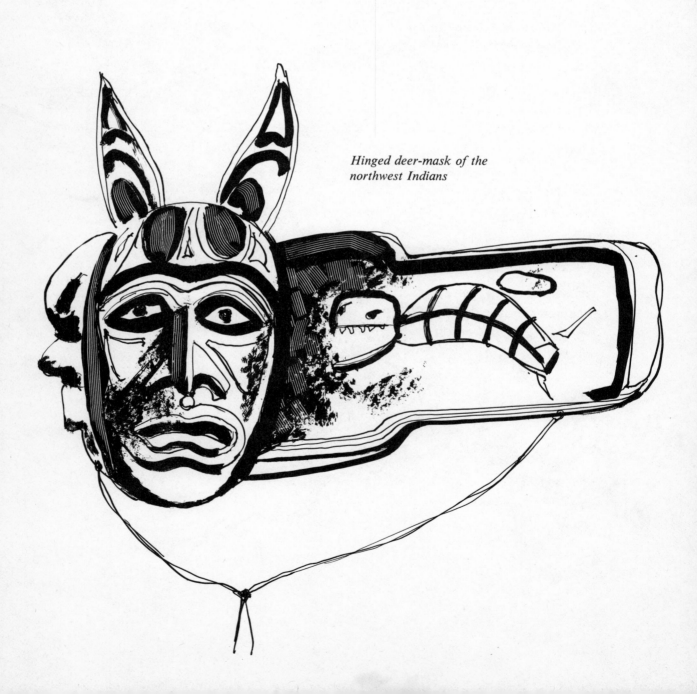

Hinged deer-mask of the northwest Indians

HAIDA

An interesting tribe of Northwest Coast Indians residing in Canada were the Haida of British Columbia. This tribe lived on two large islands and a number of small islands off the coast of what is now British Columbia. These two large islands and the smaller islands are the Queen Charlotte Islands. The annual rainfall of 60 inches, with more rainy than clear days each year, provides excessive humidity.

The days are long in summer and short in winter because of the northern location. The Japanese Current keeps the climate mild.

The forests contain hemlock, spruce, and cedar with underbrush of berry-bearing bushes. The bird life included wild ducks, geese and many others. Black bears, deer, otters, and other animals were plentiful. Sea and river life, most abundant, included shellfish, whales, halibut, cod, and salmon. The Haida were a powerful but graceful people with a coppery-tone complexion. Their broad heads and faces, their black hair, and little hair on the face and body distinguished them from other Indians.

The Haidas had a calendar that divided the year into twelve months according to the phases of the moon. Each morning at dawn when the first ray of sunshine entered a knot hole on the eastern wall of a house and shown on the opposite wall they marked that spot with a charcoal mark. When the marks again started to go in the opposite direction they knew that a half year had elapsed.

For food they gathered clams, mussels, and crabs when the tide was out. They dried certain seaweed and pressed it into cakes for the winter. The inner bark from alder and spruce was steamed and molded into cakes also for the winter. The women and children gathered huckleberries, cranberries, sala berries and other varieties of berries which were then dried as a means of preserving them. A considerable portion of their food came from the sea and included sea otters, seals, and sea lions. They were good fishermen and caught cod and dogfish.

Salmon and halibut were their main foods. The salmon were caught in dragnets or with spears. Halibut, although very large, were caught with hook and line. These fish were preserved by the women who cut them in long strips, hung them in the sun to dry or smoked them over a slow fire. Oil and grease was used as a sauce for most everything they ate. Dried foods were soaked, boiled, or dipped in oil or grease before they were eaten.

These Indians had three meals a day, which was not true of all Indians. For breakfast they would have dried halibut and boiled seaweed at dawn. They ate a big dinner just before noon and a hearty supper at about six or seven o'clock in the evening. Men and women ate together sitting cross-legged on the floor. Food was placed on wooden platters that were set on a large mat. Each person ate with a large wooden or horn spoon. The hands and face were washed and the mouth cleansed before each meal. A drink of water followed every salty course of food.

When guests came to dinner the hostess cooked and the host served. Neither ate with their guests. More food than could be eaten was cooked. Then the leftover food was sent home with the guests. The next day the guest returned the washed platters that had held the food. Sometimes presents were placed on the platters that were returned.

The Haida lived in large rectangular buildings grouped together to form villages. These were usually placed in one row facing the beach and located a few feet above high water. A house was usually about forty feet long and thirty feet wide. The roof sloped from about ten feet in the center to six feet at the sides. This roof frame rested on from six to ten large posts set deep into the ground. The roof itself placed on the frame was made of planks or bark. A hole in the center of the roof allowed for the escape of smoke from the cooking fire and for daylight. There were no windows. Cedar planks set vertically formed the walls. Houses of this type have lasted well over fifty years.

28

A Haida totem pole was often sixty feet high with an oval entrance to the house in it.
A totem was a sort of family coat-of-arms depicting history and legends of the family.

The most important and interesting part of each home was the great totem pole. This totem pole was placed in the center of the front of the house. Sometimes it was as high as sixty feet. A hole in the bottom of the totem pole sometimes served as a door to the house. Carved and painted on this pole could be found the totemic crest of the owner and his wife. Other poles commemorating special events were also found through the village, making it look like a forest of masks.

When a person entered one of these houses he would notice carved and painted poles on either side. Beside these were kept paddles, weapons, and fishing tackle. Against the wall to the left would be piled firewood. Against the wall to the right would be stored boxes of grease, berries, fish eggs, and other moist foods. The beds which were raised plank platforms covered with mats and furs were placed in the back. Also in the back would be stored boxes of dishes, clothing, blankets, dried fish and seaweed. A fire burned in a pit in the center of the floor. Covering the floor around the pit would be mats of woven design.

Few people have ever equaled the Haida as canoe builders. They

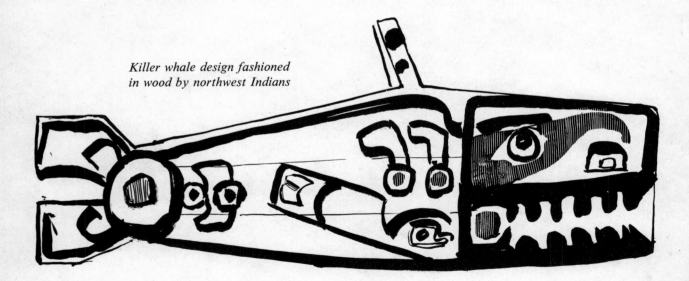

Killer whale design fashioned in wood by northwest Indians

had canoes for every purpose at sea or on the streams. Some were for work and others were for ceremonial purposes. In all, the records show that they had seven distinctly different kinds of canoes. Each type was hollowed from a single log. The largest of their canoes, seventy feet long and eight feet wide, could carry thirty men and a three-ton load. Normally the canoes were steered and propelled by paddles. When the weather was right, sails were sometimes used.

In addition to the fine houses and canoes that they made out of wood, their woodworking included spoons, platters, and boxes. All of these were made by the use of very simple tools, such as stone or iron knives, and then polished with dogfish skins.

Clothing consisted partly of garments woven from vegetable fibers and partially of furs and skins. Both men and women wore a shirt that reached to the waist. The men wore a breechclout and the women, a long skirt. Men wore cloaks of fur and women wore cloaks of tanned skins. In wet weather everyone wore a circular raincoat with a hole in the center for the head. This coat was made of fiber cloth. Everyone went barefoot and usually bareheaded.

The women wore their hair long, parted in the middle, with braids down the back. The men wore their hair loose and cut off just below their shoulders. Both sexes used scented bear grease on their hair. For ornaments they used to string together necklaces of shells, teeth, and objects of bone and copper. Persons of high rank wore bracelets and armlets of bone.

The Haidas decorated practically everything that they made. Most of the designs represented animals. Animal forms were painted on the face, woven into fabrics, carved on utensils, etched on copper, and carved and painted on houses and totem poles. On ceremonial occasions they painted designs in blue, black, and vermilion.

These Indians had no unified government. The tribe was divided into two groups known as moieties. One group was known as the Ravens and the other, Eagles. Each moiety was subdivided into about twenty clans.

Land belonged to the clan and was held in trusteeship by the chief. The Haidas rarely traded among themselves. However, they did trade a great deal with tribes on the mainland.

Local exchange of property and improvement of social position was achieved by means of a ceremony known as a potlatch. Funeral potlatches were given to hold a social position when one inherited a title from a deceased person. House-building potlatches were given when a man wanted to acquire a position through his own efforts.

It took about ten years to collect enough property to hold a house-building potlatch. This kind of property included furs, blankets, dishes, copper plates, and slaves. A year before the potlatch ceremony the wife would lend furs, blankets and other items to members of her clan. At the potlatch the borrowers returned twice the value of the items that were lent to them the year before. Just as winter set in, the host issued invitations to all persons of the opposite moiety, of his wife, to participate in the ceremony. The guests were welcomed with a big dance and then remained all winter to work for the host. The guests were entertained by clansmen of the hostess who gave feasts and dances at night throughout the period of house-building.

During the days of the weeks or months that it took to build the house the visitors were assigned specific jobs to do, such as gathering timbers, erecting the house or carving the totem pole. After the house was completed and the totem pole erected a special day was reserved for tattooing the children of the host and hostess. Other children of the hostess' moiety were also tattooed, but in this case their parents had to pay for it.

When the time of the actual potlatch arrived the guests were seated in the new house according to rank. In the back of the house the property to be given away was hidden by a curtain made of sails. Since parents paid for the tattooing of their children and borrowers returned their loans with interest this increased the pile of property.

When the curtain was thrown back the host and hostess could be seen before the pile of property, dressed in ceremonial clothes.

Haida chief with a potlatch canoe

They then gave privileged names to their children and explained where all the gifts came from. Then the hostess or host called out the ceremonial names of their guests and gave them their share of the property. The most important guests would receive slaves and coppers while someone such as a water boy would get a blanket. At the end of the potlatch the host and hostess would have nothing left but the house that had just been built. Sometimes the property that they gave away would be worth thousands of dollars. The host ended up with a house and became a house chief which gave him a great deal of prestige.

Nootka ceremonial totems

NOOTKA

One of the most interesting Indian tribes of the Northwest Coast is the Nootka of Vancouver Island, British Columbia, Canada. "Nootka" is what Captain Cook, an early sea captain explorer, thought he heard these Indians call themselves.

Because of the relatively warm climate and heavy rainfall of Vancouver Island the forests have strong growths of hemlock, fir, and cedar. Berries and edible roots were plentiful. Big game included elk, deer, and bear. Waterfowl such as duck, geese, heron, and grouse were plentiful.

The sea and streams were perhaps the greatest resource. In the fall the Indians trapped enough salmon to last them all year. Shellfish were gathered from the shore waters and fish were caught in both the ocean and rivers.

In 1939 the Nootka consisted of about 6,000 people who spoke the Nootkan language.

When the whites first traded with the Nootka it was for sea-otter. As the sea-otter were killed off contact was less frequent. Modern trading posts were then set up and white settlers and missionaries moved in. It was not long then before Nootkans began to work in the fish canneries that were opened up.

Not much is known about the Nootka before 1870 but from then until 1900 we have quite a bit of information. At this time these Indians were acquiring white settlers' implements and ideas, and working these in with their older aboriginal patterns of life.

The most important aboriginal devices were those used in the catching of salmon. A system of nets was used to guide the salmon into large cylindrical traps as they made their way up the river to spawn. The dog salmon was the most important. In order to have fish throughout the entire year the fish were dried, smoked, and stored by pressing them together and baling them. Salmon eggs were pressed into boxes and smoked into a cheese-like mass. Thus, they were sure of at least some food for the winter.

The men usually wore ornaments. In cold weather a robe of woven bark was used. During the rainy season a bark cape and cone-shaped hat provided some protection. Women always wore an apron of shredded cedar bark cloth and in cold or wet weather wore robes similar to the men's.

Men wore their hair shoulder length and women made theirs in two braids with the ends tied together. Both men and women painted their faces and used earrings and nose ornaments. In addition, women wore bead and shell necklaces, bracelets, and anklets.

Extra-special clothing and jewelry was worn during the ceremonials. At this time carved masks and headdresses, representing the heads of animals, were also worn.

Like other Northwest Coast Indians the Nootka were good carpenters even before the event of steel tools. The trees of the Pacific Northwest were turned into wooden houses, furniture, canoes, containers, and masks.

Their plank houses were very large, from 40 to 100 feet long and 30 to 40 feet wide. The houses were set in permanent frames, one located at the summer village and the other at the winter village. Two separate villages were maintained so as to be near both the summer and winter fishing sites. Sometimes the boards from the sides were moved from one home to the other as the family moved with the change in season. Each home provided shelter for a number of families closely related to the oldest male. Each of the smaller family units had its own cooking hearth and low plank beds.

Women did the family cooking although the young men did the cooking for the great feasts. Cooking was a simple process. Fresh fish was broiled over an open fire while dried fish and fresh meat were boiled in wooden boxes by dropping red-hot stones into the water-filled box. Sometimes clams, fresh fish and meat were steamed in seaweed. Whale or dogfish oil was served in separate containers in which individual pieces of food could be dipped before they were eaten.

The oldest son succeeded his father as head of the family. In

36

Nootka Indians were great whale hunters. They went after the killer whale in a huge dugout canoe. Sealskin floats helped them keep track of a harpooned whale.

Nootkan society the older persons were more important than the younger ones, and men were more important than women.

Hunting, fishing and gathering grounds were under the regulations of individuals. However, the governing person allowed his relations to benefit from the area he controlled.

In this society every member had a ranking position, that is, no two persons in a family ranked the same. Each person had a different degree of importance. In addition to the tribe members there were some slaves that were captives from other tribes. Slaves were the property of their captors and performed drudgery and degrading tasks around the camps. One had to be wealthy to have slaves as the slaves did not produce income.

Nootkas working on a whale after the catch

The more important an individual the more ornaments he could wear, and the fancier clothes he could have. In some cases he would also be given a special name. The more important the chief the more land he ruled.

Persons benefiting from a chief's lands would give him some of the products from it. The more they had the more they would give. These gifts would not really benefit the chief personally for in turn he would distribute them to members of his group during a festival or to members of another group at a feast given in their honor. The idea was to give away as much as possible. The more you had the more you could give away and therefore the more important you could become. The formal gift giving or gift exchange is known as a potlatch.

Potlatches were the high points of the social life. It was during these potlatches that persons moved up in rank.

The Nootka loved their children and were very patient with them. Children never received physical punishment. If they did wrong they were patiently corrected over and over again.

Marriages were arranged by the parents of the boy and girl. They were really marriages between families for each family tried to have their children marry someone of importance and wealth. The children had nothing to say about whom they married.

*Canoe paddles were carved
from wood*

COAST SALISH

The Salish were canoe people and excellent seamen. This was of particular importance as they lived on islands on the seashore of the coast of British Columbia, Canada. The major island was Vancouver Island. The temperature was moderate throughout the year. This meant that rivers did not freeze over and could be navigated. It rained a great deal in the winter, but was very dry during the summer.

The basic food of the Coast Salish, as was true for many of the other Northwest Indian groups, was salmon. Herring, halibut, and smelt were also plentiful. Bears, deer, wolves, land otters, and goats were found on the islands and mainland.

Fir trees were plentiful. Because it was so easy to work, the red cedar was most important to the Coast Salish. Spruce, hemlock, and juniper trees were found in various places. The cherry and crab apple provided fruit. The willow was important for basket material. Of importance to the food supply were a variety of berries, Oregon grapes, currants, and wild onions.

Two types of plank houses were used by the Coast Salish. The shed, usually used all year by the unimportant people and as a summer house only by the better class people; and the gable house, used in the winter by the wealthy and important people. The shed was very simple. It was built of four posts. Those in back were shorter than those in front. Timbers were fitted from the high to the low posts. These determined the length of the house, which was usually about sixty feet. Poles were lashed at intervals on these beams across the width of the house. Roof planks were laid on top of these poles. The walls were also of broad planks, about three feet wide, and were smooth and flat. These boards were lashed to the posts in an overlapping way similar to shingles.

The gabled house was made of a ridgepole supported by a number of posts at the ends and down the center. This formed the center and highest part of the roof. Then beams, supported on shorter posts, were placed at the edge of the house parallel to the ridgepole. These were joined by means of many rafters set in the ridgepole and the parallel beams. The roof planks, which were as long and wide as possible, were laid on top of these poles. Long, wide boards were hung on the sides in the same way the boards were fastened on the shed sides.

Both of these buildings had front and rear doors. The front door usually faced the beach. The doors were rectangular or oval in shape. Some of them swung on wooden hinges placed at the top while other doors were simply plugs that were lifted in place. To insulate the house, the inside was hung with rush mats.

A platform about three-feet wide and resting on short posts ran along all four walls. This was used for sleeping, sitting, and for storage of valuables, tools, and utensils. At appropriate places, the platform was portioned off for use by individual families. Wood was stored under it. Sections used for sleeping were provided with overhead coverings of mats or boards for warmth and to keep out the dirt. Racks placed over the bed overhead coverings were used for additional storage space.

In the larger houses, fires were in the corners and around the sides. The narrow houses had their fires down the center. Each family had its own individual fire. Drying frames were hung from the ceiling or placed on posts over the family fires.

Narrow platforms were built in front of the houses of wealthy men and were used as stages for potlatch ceremonies. The ground in front of this would be cleared down to the beach. These wealthier homes would have carved or painted crest figures or animal heads above the door or on the ends of the ridgepole or beams.

Stockades of half-logs surrounded a few villages as a protective device if natural protection was not possible.

The custom of sweating was not very important among the coast Salish, however some small sweat-houses were built and used.

Summer homes ranged from the shed just described to simple

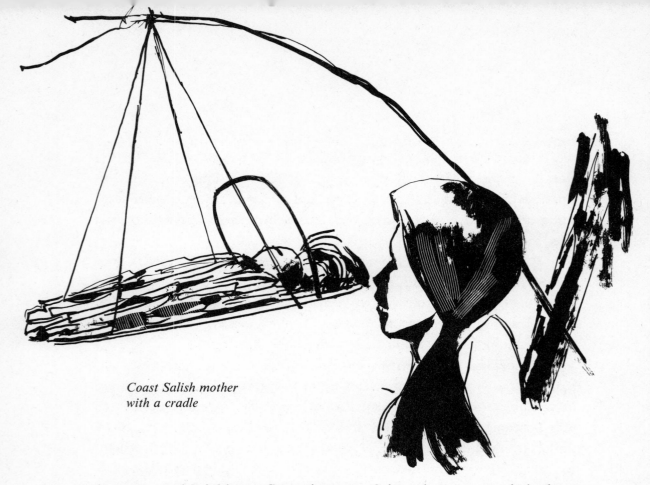

*Coast Salish mother
with a cradle*

lean-tos and wickiups. Sometimes roof boards were carried about from one temporary shelter to another.

Although four or more families usually lived in one house they operated separately and each had, in addition to its own fire, its own supply of food and other possessions. Good luck on a hunt or fishing trip was usually shared with other families living in the house. Because nobody wanted to be considered stingy they would distribute as much food as possible to other families in the house as soon as they had provided enough for their own use. When everybody had surplus food, it was preserved for use at a later date when food was not abundant.

Each family usually prepared two meals a day around its own fire. One meal was in the morning and the other was in the evening. The family members would sit around the fire on mats and eat dry food from other mats. The hands were used as utensils for dry food which made up most of the regular diet. The principal dry foods were

42

salmon, clams, and fish eggs. These were usually dipped in seal, porpoise, or fish oil that had been poured into large clam shells.

Other foods were used according to the season and luck in obtaining them. Wooden bowls were used for visitors. At the end of each meal, bowls of water and frayed bark napkins were passed around so that each person might clean his mouth and hands.

Cooking was done in one of three ways. The most common way was to put the meat or fish directly on the hot coals or fasten it on a stick that was stuck in the ground so that the meat or fish hung over the fire.

The second way was steaming. In this way heated stones were placed in a shallow pit and then covered with fresh leaves, fern, or kelp. The meat or fish was put in and another layer of leaves or seaweed put on top. The entire preparation was then covered with mats or dirt. Steam generating inside did the cooking which took overnight or longer. This earth oven was used out-of-doors, usually on the beach. Whole seals and deer were cooked this way, along with roots and bulbs. Clams were steamed open in this manner, hung above beds of coals to roast, trampled on in between two mats to make them tender, and then strung on long strings. These were worn around the neck and eaten as desired.

The third way of preparing food was by boiling. This was done by dropping hot stones in a wooden box containing the food to which water had been added. The stones were carried with wooden tongs and dipped in another box of water to clean them before being put in the cooking box. As the stones cooled in the cooking box they were removed and replaced by heated stones.

Fat from the seal, the porpoise, and the dogfish was rendered in a boiler with hot rocks in this same way. This was then skimmed off and stored in the stomach sacks of seals or sea lions that had been emptied and cleaned. Salmon, halibut, cod, and fresh meat were dried for winter use. They were cut into long slabs, dried in the sun, and then cured in a smoke house.

Other foods such as shell fish, ducks, squids, skates, deer, elk, bears, cougars, raccoons, sea gulls and eagles were eaten after either roasting, steaming, or boiling. Reptiles, owls, dogfish, sharks, ravens, killer whales, minks and wolves were never eaten. Some people would not eat a bear because it was so much like a man.

Roots, bulbs, and clams were dug with a straight, plain digging stick. The inner bark of the maple, alder, and hemlock was eaten. To get it, the outer bark was first split off. Then the inner layer was scraped off and eaten.

Berries of all kinds were preserved by boiling and then drying. Boiling was done by means of hot stones. The boiled material was poured in bark molds to dry. Another way was to mash the berries, pour in molds, and let them dry in the sun. All of these were then stored in chests. Before being eaten, they were soaked in water.

Red cedar was used for making chests, boxes, and pails. The best wood for spoons, dishes, and bowls was maple. These were all carved. In many cases the ends of spoons and long bowls had animal designs carved on them. Dishes were not used individually. They were filled with food and spaced among those eating. Food was then taken from them by individuals.

In the summer old men went naked or wore a blanket over their shoulders. Young and middled-aged men wore a belt that had a front apron attached to it. Women wore a knee-length skirt of wool, skin, or bark that was fastened in place by a belt. In the winter and on special occasions buckskin clothes were worn. Shirts for men had sleeves and were made in two pieces, a front and back, sewn together. Men also wore trousers of knee or ankle length. Women wore a sleeved, knee-length buckskin gown. Shirts and gowns were fastened down the front with bone pins.

For an outer garment both men and women wore a robe thrown over the shoulders. A belt drew it close about the waist. The skins of the bear, the wildcat, the raccoon, the deer, the cougar, and the marten were used. Blankets were made of twined, frayed bark, wool,

The Coast Salish Indians sometimes steamed
food. Heated stones in a pit were covered with
seaweed. Fish, a seal or a whole deer was
put in the pit and covered with more seaweed.
Then covered with mats or dirt it steamed
all night.

or wool and duck down. Sleeveless jackets, made of sealskin or twined cedar bark, were worn by both men and women. Moccasins were used in cold and snowy weather.

Men cut their hair shoulder length and parted it in the middle. Women did their hair in two braids on either side of the head. Combs carved out of wood were used by both men and women.

Both men and women wore nose and ear ornaments on special occasions. When an infant was a few weeks old the septum of the nose and lobe of the ears were pierced to provide holes for this purpose. The holes would be kept open with pendants or wool yarn until the child grew up.

The food-getting occupations of hunting, fishing, and gathering used up most of the time of the men and women. This was particularly true from March until November when most of the food was secured and preserved. From November until March other activities such as woodworking, canoe making, weaving, basket making, and skin dressing filled up their time.

Fish were caught by means of traps, harpoons, hand nets, and hooks. The greatest quantity of fish was caught in the spring. Most hunting was done in the summer and fall. Hunting was done at night by two persons in a canoe. One would hold a torch and, when an animal came down to the water's edge to look at it, the other would shoot it with a bow and arrow. Dogs were used to track down deer, goat and bear.

Everyone knew something of woodworking. However, some men became specialists in weapons, house planks, or canoes. Women made their own yarn and wove blankets and clothing from it. Some baskets were made but this art was not developed as much as some of the others mentioned.

Supernatural helpers were considered most essential to hunters, fishermen, and canoe makers. Thus, every man tried to get a spirit helper of some sort. To do this, all boys, and girls to some extent, went through a hard course of training. This prepared them for a

46

supernatural experience where they became acceptable to the animal spirit that would help them. Usually the boy received a song, learned how to paint his face, and was given permission to use the animal's cry.

Heads were deformed in infancy by binding a cedar-bark pad tightly against the forehead with a strap tied to the sides of the cradle. The head would rest on a pad or pillow. As a result the head would grow flat at the front and back. This made the head beautiful according to this group of Indians.

A deformed head was a mark of beauty among Coast Salish Indians

TSIMSHIAN

The Tsimshian Indians lived along the banks and tributaries of the Nass and Skeena Rivers in British Columbia. The seacoast and coastal islands in this area also belonged to them. They ranged from the coastal islands and seacoast to the river basins on both sides of the coastal range of mountains. This meant that they were familiar with a variety of living conditions and became both mountain and sea dwellers. This was unusual for the other Indian tribes, like the Haida, were only seaside dwellers.

Heavy rainfall on the coastal side of the mountains provided water for streams and lakes. Fish such as salmon and eulachon were plentiful. The temperature was moderate throughout the year. Very little snow fell in the winter time. Large forests contained cedar, spruce, fir and hemlock. Marshes were deep with layers of wet spongy mosses.

North and east of the coastal range the land was drier and much better for hunting. Here there were no dense forests but there were large sections of alder, maple, spruce and birch.

Since it was possible to travel on both the Nass and Skeena rivers by canoe, the Tsimshian had a good travel route from the coast to the inter-mountain plateaus.

The Tsimshian language is quite distinctive from other Indian languages. In fact, men who study languages have not been able to determine how it was developed nor if there are any other languages like it. Three different dialects were spoken, but they were similar and the people speaking them could understand each other.

In the winter the Tsimshian lived in villages on the banks of streams or alongside the ocean beaches. In the 1800's about twenty-five villages were known by traders and travelers. Those located on rivers were either on the Nass or Skeena, except for the village of Kitwinkool which was on the Kitwinkool River.

Permanent villages usually had less than one hundred people. If possible, villages were located on points of land jutting out into the

48

The raven, considered a sacred bird by many tribes of Northwest Indians, was often featured in the ceremonial dances.

water with forests or swamps in the back. This was for protection. It was also necessary to have a good beach for the landing of canoes as they were the chief means of transportation.

Houses were built to face the stream or ocean and if enough clear land was available were built in one row. The houses had to be in a well-drained location as the floors were of earth or sand. These low-gabled plank houses were usually made of cedar planks and were rectangular in shape.

The family cooking fires were in the middle of the house. Surrounding the fires could be found firewood, smooth stones for food boiling and various cooking and serving utensils and dishes. A platform along the walls served as beds, seats, and shelves for storing the families' possessions. Goods were kept in large, painted or carved chests. Dried foods were hung up in the beams of the house where they were kept dry by the heat of the fire. Other foods were stored in boxes that were buried in the ground. Since the ground was cool it kept the food from spoiling.

The back of the house was reserved for the house head, his family, and possessions. The side compartments were assigned nephews, brothers, or other close male relatives and their families. Slaves with their few possessions lived in the coldest sections of the house, which were on either side of the door. Chiefs had larger houses because they entertained more and held public meetings there.

When the Tsimshian saw how the whites, who had come into the territory, built houses they soon added windows, and replaced door coverings with hinged doors. They also began to use milled lumber. The interior design was changed to include a high-ceilinged family room with a number of small sleeping and storage rooms off to the sides.

Tsimshian families built smokehouses and cabins at the hunting and fishing camps. These cabins were sometimes just temporary shelters of bark or mat lean-tos instead of plank cabins.

Canoes provided the primary means of transportation on the

many rivers and on the ocean. These canoes were made of extremely large cedar logs. These logs were first shaped and hollowed out. Next, the canoe was filled with water that was heated by adding hot stones. This softened the wood which could then be stretched. Logs were used to force the canoe to a wider and proper shape. Some of these canoes were so large and so well made that they could convey three tons of material.

Those Tsimshian who lived on or traveled up the smaller streams used small dugouts or bark canoes. When traveling in the high country in the winter, where considerable snow was likely to be found, they used snowshoes.

Salmon was the major food of the Tsimshian. Three different varieties, Cohoes, Sockeye, and Humpbacks were dried for winter use. Eulachon, a kind of candlefish that contained a great deal of oil, was one of the important foods. Herring, cod, and halibut were also important in their diet.

Bear, deer, and mountain goat were all hunted for food and for their skins. Hair seals, sea lions, and seals were also hunted. Berries were plentiful and used a great deal. They not only used shellfish and seaweed for food for themselves, but traded it to other tribes living inland. Because they knew the various ways of preserving food by drying, smoking, rendering oil from fish and sealing foods in fat, they were able to preserve the various foods when they were plentiful and have a good supply on hand for times when they were not.

The head of each household had the right to the use of certain areas of land and water for the purpose of hunting, fishing, and gathering food and raw materials. These rights were passed down from father to son. Each clan had a hereditary leader. The Tsimshian heir was the eldest son of the chief's eldest sister. If an area was unoccupied or had been abandoned, anyone could claim it and start to use it. Chiefs and heads of families determined when their extended family moved from one seasonal camp to another. These heads also determined how much food was to be preserved and supervised the work being done. The Tsimshian were divided into four groups which controlled marriage and descent: Eagles, Wolves, Ravens, and Killer Whales.

Feasts, potlatches, and the building of a new house were planned years in advance as it took a long time to collect the necessary food and materials required. Spring and summer were the busy seasons when food was preserved. It was also during the summer season that materials were collected for household furnishings, tools, clothing and buildings. Not much food was available during the stormy months from November through February. It was during this winter season that entertaining, feasting, trading, potlatching, and house-building took place.

Some villages tended to specialize in one kind of activity and traded their products to others. Those who lived on the coast traded oil and seaweed for wool, fat, and horn to those who lived in the mountains. Many men specialized in woodcraft and, in addition to canoes, made boxes, masks and totem poles.

The Tsimshian were very good in all of the arts. They were excellent musicians, dancers and dramatists. Large box drums and wooden rattles were the major instruments. They had songs for every occasion. These songs were treasured because it was believed that they were gifts from supernatural beings. In turn they were handed down from father to son. Song contests were common. Dramatics were of great interest and many performances were put on.

Men carved, painted, and sculptured. In addition to the usual wood, they worked in bone, stone, horn, and copper. For daily use they made chests, dishes, trays, boxes, spoons, fishhooks and clubs in addition to the canoes for which they were famous. For special occasions they carved and painted rattles, drums, headdresses, and masks. The most spectacular product was the carved and painted totem pole. Interior villages of the Tsimshian sometimes had totem poles more than 50 feet high in front of their houses. Copper was used for arrow heads, daggers, ornaments, and as inlay in wood.

52

The women did the weaving and made the clothing. The Tsimshian women made what was known as a Chilkat robe. This was woven from yarn made by twisting mountain-goat wool and yellow-cedar bark together. Men usually made the designs for the women to follow in their weaving.

Both the Tsimshian men and women on the coast wore small skin aprons fastened front and back to a belt. On rainy or cold days robes or blankets made of cedar bark, fur, or dressed skins were worn. Those in the interior wore dressed skin clothing, fur robes and moccasins. Their shirts, leggings, and women's robes were somewhat fitted and held together with tie strings.

Halibut hook, suspended from a hand-hold with a thong

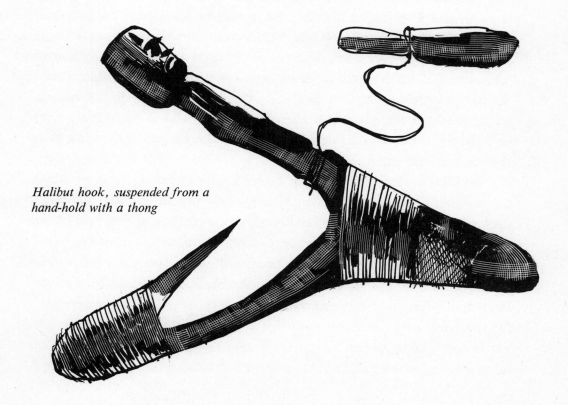

OKINAGAN

The Okinagan Indians were a Salish-speaking people of north-central and eastern Washington, British Columbia, Idaho, and western Montana. Although these Indians did not live on the Pacific coast they were near enough so that they were influenced by the west coast Indians.

The foods of the Okinagan were similar to the other Indians of the plateau area. They used every variety of fish, game, root, and berry that was available. In addition they also used moss, seeds, and the cambium layer of pine trees.

During the winter time most of the people lived in a long house or underground house in one of the villages. Those who had not put up a large supply of food for the winter had to go on frequent hunting trips to secure food. Bears were caught in March and April.

During the latter part of April fish known as "suckers" would start to run in from the ocean and would be caught in traps. Then in June the salmon run would begin and salmon could be caught until October. This meant that the Indians had to leave their winter homes and camp near the river beds where they did the fishing. Semi-permanent camps were set up during this season. Early in the spring, while the men fished, the women dug camas roots, bitterroot, wild carrots, wild onions, and potatoes. It was also during the spring that the women collected berries.

In October the fall hunting started. The men hunted deer while the women stayed in camp cutting and drying the meat. Although deer meat was preferred, probably equal quantities of fish and plant products were eaten. Winter homes were then built or repaired and all were settled for the winter by the middle of November. Each year the pattern was just about the same, for each family usually went to the same fishing and hunting grounds and returned to its own village for the winter.

Food was stored in many ways. Some was stored in the woods on frames eight feet above the ground so as to be out of the reach of animals. Rock shelters and pits in the ground were used. On arrival at the winter village, food was stored in the houses or kept in pits near by.

In the early days underground houses were common but later the mat-covered lodge for winter and the mat-covered tipi for summer were used. The mat-covered lodge was oblong with an "A" shaped roof that came all the way to the ground. The framework was of poles covered with woven mats, except for a long slit in the top that let the smoke from the fire escape. The framework consisted of a series of pairs of poles spread apart at the bottom and tied together at the top. For support a cross pole was tied about one third of the way down. The side frame poles were tied in such a way as to hold the upright poles in place. One end faced south and this end had a door.

If the house was very long, say forty feet, a door might also have been built on the north end. Mats were placed on the pole frames in much the same way shingles are placed. Four or five layers of mats were used on the bottom rows and one on the top row. Sunlight could go through the top row, but rain could not.

Each long mat lodge was used by a number of families. Each family had its own section. Food was stored up in the eaves and just inside the door. Each family had its own fire. This meant a series of fires down the middle of the lodge.

In summer the mats were rolled up and stored in trees or carried to the summer camp and used on the mat-tipi shelters. The mat-covered tipi was built with a foundation of three or four long poles and filled in by a number of shorter poles. Branches were wound around the frames and the mats were put on the same way as shingles. Long heavy poles were placed on the outside to hold the mats in place. Storage space was again provided just inside the entrance and there was a smoke hole, the same as in the mat lodge. Since the tipis were about ten feet in diameter, only one or two families could live in one.

At one time clothing probably consisted of a bark breechclout for the men and bark skirt for the women. Just prior to the coming of the white men, buckskin, thin in the summer and thick in the winter, was in general use. The men wore a breechclout and belt, moccasins, long leggings, shirt, and a cap or headband. The women wore either a long dress, or a shirt and skirt, moccasins, and short leggings. In warm weather the men and children would remove their shirts and leggings. Deer skins and the skins of the wolf, fox, coyote and otter were used for clothing. Children wore the same type of clothing as adults of the same sex.

Men wore their hair in two braids hanging in front of the ears, and in front of the shoulders. The front hair was cut off at about the level of the eyebrows and combed straight back. Women parted their hair in the middle and had two braids hanging down the back of their neck. Sometimes the braids were tied together in front or on the back of the neck. Both men and women would place bits of fur into their braids. Porcupine quills were also used for hair decorations. Women greased their hair to make it look better. Soap for washing the hair and body was made by soaking dogwood leaves in cold water for an hour to produce a lather. In order to have soap all year, dogwood leaves would be collected in August and stored for later use. Men plucked out their facial hairs.

Bows and arrows were the major weapons. Bows four to five feet long were made of cedar, dogwood, or maple. Bow strings were made of deer leg sinew or two thicknesses of hemp rolled together. Arrows used for hunting were about three-and-a-half feet long. War arrows were about a foot shorter. Serviceberry wood, which was a kind of cane, was used for the shaft. These arrows were feathered with three vanes of eagle, grouse or hawk feathers. For small game the shafts were sharpened to a point. When used for large game or war, arrowheads of bone or flint were used.

Clubs were made out of pieces of deer horn or stone. They were usually about two feet long.

A single knife served for all purposes. It was of flint stone, shaped and sharpened by flaking off the edges until one edge was shaped properly. Then it was smoothed by rubbing on a rough stone. One end was wrapped with buckskin.

Spears of various lengths were used. Those used for deer were about ten feet long and had a bone or flint head. Spears were not thrown but thrust into the animal without losing hold of the shaft. Hide shields were used in warfare.

The canoes were made chiefly of yellow pine, but sometimes of cedar or cottonwood. They varied in length from twelve to thirty feet and were two-feet wide. A boat could hold ten or twelve people. Single-end paddles about four or five feet long were used.

Coiled baskets made of cedar root bark were used for storage, cooking, and berry gathering. They were made in all sizes and shapes.

Twined bags with round bottoms were made of Indian hemp or wild hop-vine bark.

Birchbark buckets were made of a single rectangular piece of bark. Green bark was used and was so cut that the sides and bottom came out of the same piece. The ends were folded and laced together with Indian hemp twine. These birchbark buckets were used for carrying and storing a variety of materials.

Measuring was done in relation to the length of the various parts of the arm, the span of the thumb and forefinger, and the width of the thumb.

Time was recorded by tying knots in a string. One knot meant one day. After one hundred knots were tied one knot was substituted for them and the counting went on. The knots representing hundreds were tied closer together than the knots representing one.

TLINGIT

The territory of the Tlingit was in Southeastern Alaska. It extended from Yakutat Bay in the north to Hecate Strait in the south, and consisted of all the offshore islands and extended inland. Because of the salt content of the water the many inlets and rivers did not freeze in the winter and could be used by boats throughout the entire year. Hot springs in the area of Sitka were used by the Indians to cure various ailments. The average temperature for the summer was 59°F and for winter 32°F. On the average it rained or snowed two hundred days a year.

Because of the heavy rainfall the vegetation grew rapidly and was very thick. Poplar, willow, birch, hemlock, and fir provided wood for various purposes. The deep forests were so damp that forest fires could not burn in them.

Wild blueberries and currants grew throughout the territory. The cold, wet climate was not suitable for grains or fruits, but cabbage, rutabagas, radishes, and peas were grown after they were acquired from Europeans.

Bears were very plentiful. The fox, wolf, land otter and ermine were also found. The most valuable fur-bearing animal was the sea otter. Small game included the squirrel, rabbit, and porcupine. Birds were also plentiful including the raven which was a sacred bird among the Tlingit.

Fish was the most important food. And salmon was the most plentiful. Salmon were caught in the rivers during the summer when they went up the rivers to spawn. They were caught with hooks, spears, and traps. The most common means was the trap which was actually a fence of basketry which directed the fish into a basket trap. To preserve the salmon, they were cleaned and hung up to dry. Then they were tied up in bundles and stored for later use. Various kinds of fish could be caught all the year round. Other fish that were used for food included smelt, haddock, and halibut. Throughout the villages were racks used for drying fish.

Around each village would be found half-wild dogs that spent a considerable amount of their time either howling or stealing food.

Because of the climate, rainfall, and mountainous nature of the country, neither gardening nor cattle raising could be practiced.

As was usual in many Indian groups, these Indians called themselves "the people." In this case the word for "the people" was *Tlingit*, hence these Indians are known as the Tlingit. The Tlingit consisted of many tribes, each tribe living in a separate village quite far from its neighbor.

During the winter they lived in villages but in the summer they scattered according to clan or family, to hunt, fish, or trade. The Tlingit villages were an impressive sight as seen from across the water for they poked out of the wilderness as if they had been transplanted there. The shore line would be covered with piles of fishing gear and canoes in back of which would be a row of wooden houses. Totem poles or grave posts, sticking out here and there, added color. Because of the importance of fishing, villages were always close to good fishing grounds. Villages varied in size from a few houses to sixty or more. Paths led from one house to another and from each house to the forest where firewood could be collected. The houses, which were built near the shore, had the door side facing the water.

The houses were built on four great posts that had been sunk in the ground at the four corners. Beams were fitted in for the roof and side walls, and then boards fastened on the sides and roof. Bark was used as wedges between the boards if the fit was not perfect. The only opening was the doorway which had either a mat covering or a square strong wood door. The cooking fire was in the middle of the house. The Tlingit had totem poles but did not use them as much as their neighboring tribes.

Outside the row of houses were other houses set up on poles. These were grave houses which contained the ashes of cremated bodies.

The Tlingit themselves were of medium height, well built, and strong. Although most of the men walked tall most of the women waddled along in a slightly bent over position. Their skin was quite light and looked more European than Indian. Their teeth were usually good and very white. The hair was pitch black turning gray in old age. The little beard they had was pulled out by the men.

Both the men and women pierced their noses in order to insert decorative rings. In addition the women also pierced their ears to add ornaments of stone, shell and teeth.

All the women had the lower lip pierced the full length of the mouth and down to the gum. In some cases this was done when they were babies and, in other cases, at about twelve years of age. Young girls would have a nail in this slit; married women wore a wooden spoon. This would cause the lip to extend. The item inserted in the lip was known as a *labret*. The women also wore many strings of beads and bracelets.

Girls wore their hair in a braid in back which might be pulled through a wooden ring much like the pony tail of today. Men wore their hair, which had been coated with grease, loose and let it fall on the neck. Older women wore their hair the same as the men, but let it grow longer and parted it in the middle. Each day they took a bath in the sea.

Inside their houses, a Tlingit squatted or lay stretched out on the floor with the head resting on one arm. Chairs or benches were not used. The fire was kept going all day. The wood necessary for the fire was collected each day by the men and boys. The principal activity of the day was the preparation and the eating of food.

The main dish was fish. This was boiled, roasted, dried, but never eaten raw. Next in importance in food, came the meat of land and sea mammals. Then came fowl, crabs, squid, and shellfish. Although not so important, but used whenever available, were plant products such as berries, roots, and bulbs.

Cooking was done in wooden vessels or in closely woven baskets

A Tlingit potlatch ceremony was a high point in the social life. With a potlatch a person moved up in rank. The more he could give away the more important he became, and the more gifts he could expect in return.

that were watertight. This was done by putting hot stones in the bowl or basket containing the fish or meat. A lid was put on top to hold in the heat. Fish and venison were stuck on wooden sticks and roasted over an open fire.

Spoons were carved from bone or wood. In general, however, the fingers were used for getting the food to the mouth. The Tlingit ate several meals a day but at no special time, except for the major meal which was usually eaten at midday. Much of the food was prepared or dipped in fish oil. A great quantity of water was drunk with each meal. Snow was eaten with pleasure all year round. In the summer it would be brought from the mountains as a special treat.

Hunting, fishing, and trapping took a good deal of the men's time. When this was not necessary they would make or repair cooking utensils, traps, canoes and other necessary items.

The women did most of the cooking, took care of the small children and made baskets and clothes. During the fishing season they preserved fish. In the fall they picked berries and collected other plant materials. Each member of the family had his own specific job responsibilities.

The Tlingit kept clean through the use of sweat baths and by plunging into the sea. They did this throughout the year, even in the winter time.

When a Tlingit gave a present he expected something in return. If given a present, he would figure that the person owed it to him or wanted something from him.

Since fish was the major food, fishing was the major occupation of these Indians. Great care was taken in the building of the canoes used for fishing. They were made during the winter of red cedar logs, if available. If cedar was not available, Sitka spruce or poplar logs were used. To get a log the tree would be partially chopped and then burned down with a fire. The outside would be shaped with an ax. The inside chopped out in the same way. To make the canoe wider, it was filled with water that was heated by dropping in hot stones. This made the wood pliable so that the sides could be spread out by forcing them apart with small logs. Canoes were made all sizes from small ones for two to three men to those forty-five feet long that held sixty-five men. The larger canoes would have a carved figure on the bow. Although they had good canoes, the Tlingit did not risk their lives in the open sea during stormy weather.

The outside of a dugout canoe was shaped with a hand ax

WISHRAM

The Wishram Indians were one of the earliest tribes known to the explorers of the Columbia River basin. Only a few Wishram still remain. Some still occupy their original home at Spedis, Washington, opposite The Dalles, while others are on the Yakima reservation in Central Washington. Originally they were a small tribe occupying the north bank of the Columbia River about The Dalles. They spoke Chinook.

It is believed that the Wishram depended primarily on fishing for their supply of food. The chief fish taken was the salmon with some pike, sturgeon, trout, and eel. Shellfish were also used. Ideal spots were available for both netting and spearing fish. Fish traps were also used. Small fish were dried whole. The salmon was dried, powdered, and then stored in baskets lined with dry salmon skin. Fresh fish was prepared by steaming.

Hunting was secondary to fishing with these Indians. Deer, elk, and bear were hunted under the direction of a hunt leader who decided when, where, and what to hunt. The game taken was divided equally among all those who were in the party. Squirrels, goats, birds, and waterfowl were also taken as the occasion permitted.

Another secondary source of food was the various plant products such as roots, berries, nuts, and seeds. The gathering was done by the women. In the spring they dug for roots with a digging stick. This was a stick about two feet long with a curved point on one end and a short cross grip on the other. Nuts were collected in the fall.

The principal method of cooking vegetables was by roasting in a pit. Boiling was a secondary means. Food was served at meals in bowls made of wood and horn. Two meals were served each day, one in the morning and the other in the evening.

Since they were a river people living on the Columbia, canoes were very important. They were built of white cedar or pine and were light and beautifully made. Some had carved figures of men and animals on the bow and stern. The leader of a canoe party sat in the

64

The Wishram Indians, who lived originally on the north bank of the Columbia River near The Dalles, fished for salmon with nets, traps or spears.

stern and steered. Three paddlers had places in front of him.

The Wishram did a lot of woodworking. In addition to the canoes they made bowls, mortars, troughs, ladles, spoons, bows, and cradleboards. For tools they had axes, chisels, wedges, and knives. Plank houses and wooden boxes made by the other Northwest Indians were not common with these people.

Awls and needles were used in the sewing of skins and in the making of coiled baskets.

Mats were woven from reeds and used on beds, floors and for roofing material.

Baskets and bags were used for moving and for storing food. Baskets, the most numerous articles in the household, were both twined and coiled. Small twined baskets, about one-half gallon to two gallon size were used in collecting nuts, berries, and roots. Larger baskets of two and a half gallons or more were used for storage. A simple basket took about two days to make. A decorated one four days.

Bows and arrows were used for small game. The bows were made of dogwood or oak. Arrows were made of any hard wood. Hides of large animals were very valuable and therefore were carefully tanned.

A few musical instruments were available. These were drums, rasps, and rattles. The drums were either a long plank, used by many drummers or a tambourine-type drum used by a single drummer. The rasp was a notched stick that was rubbed up and down with another stick. The rattle was made of deer hoofs threaded on a sinew cord that was in turn tied to a six-inch handle.

Houses were either earth lodges partially underground, usually for winter use, or a mat lodge primarily for summer use. The earth lodge was built over a pit about sixteen feet in diameter and about four feet deep. A number of families lived in a house, depending on its size. The mat lodge with a gable roof was built above ground. Small mats covered the floor except where the fireplace was located.

Before the tribe had horses, most of the materials that had to be moved were carried by the women. Loads were carried on the back by a packstrap that passed over the forehead or in front of the shoulders. Indian women would carry fish and wood in this manner. A woman that weighed 150 pounds could carry a 200 pound pack in this manner. Packstraps were braided cords or deerskin straps.

Not much is known about the clothing worn by the Wishram men and women. In all probability both wore a breechclout, a sleeveless vest, and fur robe for the winter time. Breechclouts were made of fur such as raccoon. Moccasins were also worn by both men and women. Both sexes wore their hair the same way. It was parted straight up the crown and hung in a braid in front of each shoulder. Ear pendants were also used by both sexes of the Wishram.

In Wishram society there were three classes of people in addition to the slaves. The highest class were the chiefs and their families. Next came the middle class who were not closely related to chiefs. Then there was the lower class who were poor. They had no slaves or other possessions. Slaves were captured in war or secured in trade.

Wishram Indians with simple musical instruments

MAKAH

In the northwestern corner of the state of Washington early settlers located a tribe of Indians known as the Makah. They were a happy, contented people, perhaps because they had no difficulty in securing food from both the land and the sea. On one side they had the sea and on the other the mountains. Thus, they went one way when they wanted fish and another when they wanted meat.

Three villages at Neah Bay made up the winter residence of the Makah Indians. These villages were *Wa-atch*, *Tsoo-ess*, and *Ho-sett*. During the summer months they moved to villages nearer Cape Flattery known as *Kiddleaibbut*, *Taloosh*, and *Archawat*. The purpose of the move was to be nearer the fishing grounds in the summer time.

Their houses were built of cedar boards and planks. Each board or plank was split from cedar logs by the use of little wedges. Each house was about forty to sixty feet square and eighteen to twenty feet high. Several families lived in each house and each family had its own fire. The houses were comfortable, that is, if a person could get accustomed to the smoke from all of the fires.

Most of the things that the men made were used in either hunting or fishing. They made harpoons, spears, bows, arrows, fishhooks, and fish lines. Fish lines were made by just cleaning and then tying pieces of kelp together until the line was the desired length. The women braided mats from cedar bark and wove blankets from dog hair. Baskets and conical-shaped hats were made from spruce roots, cedar twigs, and bleached bear grass.

In 1862, when they entered the reservation, Makah men and women wore blankets. In addition, the women wore a cotton or cedar bark skirt. During the rains or cold weather the men added a bearskin cloak. This bearskin cloak had the head cut off so the forepaws could be brought around the side of the neck and fastened. Both men and women had the cartilage of the nose pierced and into this was tied a piece of abalone shell. In addition to this nose ornament, shell ear pieces were also worn in pierced ears.

When doing their work such as fishing or trading they tended to be very dirty. That is, both their clothes and bodies would be covered with dirt or fish oil. On their return from trading or fishing trips they would wash themselves and their possessions. When at home they would wash every morning. They were very fond of bathing and had a daily bath, even in the coldest weather. As soon as they finished bathing they would have breakfast.

Most of the usual three meals taken each day included the same food items regardless of the time of the day they were eaten. A typical meal would include boiled duck or fish, dried halibut and whale oil. The food was served in wooden bowls and each person helped himself to what he wanted by using his fingers. On completion of the meal the face and hands would be wiped on cedar bark that had been beaten to a soft mass. Then the mouth would be rinsed with a drink of cold water.

On feast days they would go from house to house eating a meal at each house. If their stomachs got too full they would bring up the food by sticking their fingers down their throats, and then start off fresh with another meal at the next house.

Important foods were dried halibut, dried whale blubber, whale oil, and cod. Other fish and shellfish such as mussels, crabs, and clams were also used. Whale blubber was prepared by cutting it in strips, boiling it and then pouring off the oil. After boiling, the blubber was smoked and dried like bacon. The oil was boiled the second time to get rid of any water and then saved for use later on. The halibut was cut into thin flakes and dried in the sun. These halibut flakes were either eaten dry, dipped in whale oil or toasted before the fire.

The Makah were expert canoemen and went many miles out to sea in canoes to fish.

Each canoe was a work of art. It was carved from a single cedar log. When whaling, the canoe was manned by eight men. Six paddled, one steered, and the other threw the harpoon.

The Makah were very fond of music and they had many songs and chants that they sang in chorus.

Makah Indians wore a bearskin cloak in cold or rainy weather

Chapter III

INDIANS OF CALIFORNIA

ONE OF THE most interesting groups of Indian tribes are those who lived on the Pacific coast in the area now known as the state of California. In addition to the Northwest Coast Indians who occupied the coastal area reaching into northern California, and the Southwest Indians such as the Yuman speaking Indians who ranged out to the lower southern California coast, there were many tribes that occupied central and southern California. There were over sixteen different tribes in central California and many individual groups which made up what was known as the Mission Indians.

One of the most interesting things about these tribes was that among the sixteen tribes they spoke languages representing five of the major groups of the Indian language families found north of Mexico. The only one not spoken was Eskimo. Sixty different dialects have been identified. It is possible that the various tribes stopped off on the coast on their way south, or as they moved west across the continent, and some stayed on permanently while the others drifted on. Thus, the entire state was peopled with small pockets of distinctly different Indian groups. Each group was independent and hostile toward the others.

The California region is by far the smallest of the cultural areas occupied by American Indians. The rolling valley country contributed to the formation of many isolated valley communities.

The climate provided few extremes in temperature. In general, the summers were dry and the winters wet. The valleys had a good grass growth with shrubs in the foothills. The mountains were forest covered with many oak trees on the middle levels.

Most of the food animals were small and rabbits and birds were plentiful and important. There were also some deer and bear. Insects, such as locusts and grasshoppers, were collected and eaten after being roasted. Groups on the coast took advantage of the fish and shellfish, both of which were important sources of food and were used for trading. However, the California Indians were essentially an inland people and did not depend very much on the sea.

The rainfall was not adequate nor did it come at the right time for garden or field vegetables. Very few were raised as these Indians had not learned how to irrigate. Instead, they gathered and used for food acorns, seeds, fruits, and berries of all kinds.

A great diversity of Indian life was found among the various tribes that occupied central California. The population was dense even in the ancient days, for the California area was then, as now, a desirable place to live.

All of these tribes were hunters, gatherers of plants, and basket makers. California was one of the major areas of the basket-making industry in the United States. With so much vegetable material and fruits easily available these Indians had more time that could be used as they chose. They had time for making baskets, for carrying out ceremonies, and for warfare. Very fine baskets were produced and in some cases designs were worked in with beads and small feathers.

Sacramento and Fresno now occupy what was once meadows with small through-flowing streams. This was wonderful acorn country. There were fish in the rivers and small game in the fields and near-by hills.

Most of the groups preferred to keep the peace unless invaded. Many of the boundaries of territory were settled and seldom disputed in the far west.

In the winter they lived in clusters of hamlets, and they wandered in bands during the summer. Often the houses were built partly underground.

Most of the tribes cremated their dead. Many of the ceremonies

72

Acorns were a main source of food for Indians in the Sacramento and American River valleys. People sometimes owned their own trees.

centered around one of their greatest concerns, death. Various kinds of anniversaries were held for the dead.

Most of the tribes emphasized one primary God but also believed in others. Shamans, Indian medicine men, were specialists in this part of the country. They worked in witchcraft and magic. Some sucked wounds to cure, others worked to control the weather, while still others related themselves to animals to gain supernatural power from them.

Indians may have been in parts of southern California, where the Mission Indians lived, during the Ice Age, for stone tools and grinding stones from that period of time have been found in this area. If so, they probably gathered seeds as well as hunted animals for food. These California food-gatherers who lived here a long time ago left shell mounds, now believed to be at least seven thousand years old.

Since history has been written these Indians have been called Diggers as well as Mission Indians. This is because digging for roots was an important food-gathering activity. These small groups that split or strayed away from their parent groups soon lost their original identity and were named after the Spanish mission near which they lived. Thus the parent groups became depleted and also lost their identity.

This part of California provided food sources not enjoyed elsewhere. The acorn was a staple. By pounding it into a meal and then boiling the meal in a basket, by using hot stones, a kind of mush was made. The tannic acid that made the acorns bitter was first leached out by pouring boiling water over the meal that had been placed in a basket.

Some tribes made use of the coastal waters the year round. Others came yearly to trade for fish, clams, and shell money. They wandered in small groups in the summer and congregated in villages for the winter.

Most of these California Indians were converted to Christianity

74

less than two hundred years ago by the Franciscan Missionaries. The first mission, at San Diego, was founded in 1769, and the last at San Francisco, in 1823. This was just twenty-six years before the famous California gold rush. The Franciscans gathered the Indians together in villages, taught them Christianity and also taught them trades. Each mission usually consisted of a church, a school, and shops. Many Indians could not stand the confinement.

California was then a part of Mexico. When Mexico gained her independence from Spain no one was left to support the missions or care for the Indians. The Indians were helpless against the white men who crowded in around them. About a hundred years later, after California became part of the United States, small parcels of land were set aside for the various Indian groups.

*Grasshoppers were caught,
roasted and eaten*

POMO

The Pomo Indians, at the time that they were studied, which was in the early nineteen hundreds, occupied an area north of San Francisco between the ocean and the Sacramento River. It extended about one hundred and thirty miles north and south, and about one hundred miles east and west. In general, this was the area in between the two ranges of coast mountains. In these mountains were found many streams and fertile sheltered valleys. It was along these streams and in the valleys that the Pomo Indians lived. It has been estimated that at one time there were over seventy five different villages. The Pomo were among the best known Indian groups of California.

The word *pomo* means *red clay*. These Indians were called Pomo because of the value that they placed on this "red clay" for flavoring and coloring the bread that they made out of acorn flour. A small amount of this red clay was dissolved in water and mixed with the finely ground acorn flour.

The acorns and similar food supplies were kept in large storehouse baskets which stood on low scaffolds.

Although the climate was varied, it was mild. Heavy fogs were frequent in the coastal area. Both windy and rainy seasons were experienced.

Timber was plentiful throughout the entire area with dense redwood forests starting on the shore of San Francisco Bay and extending north. Douglas fir, spruce, sugar pine, and yellow pine were fairly common. The oak which was also very plentiful was most significant as it provided the acorn which was one of the staples in the Pomo Indians' diet. Various fruit trees and shrubs grew wild, including the grape. Bulbs, such as lilies, and seed from the grasses, grew abundantly and were used for food.

Deer were plentiful and formed one of the chief sources of meat for these people. Other animals that were killed for food included the black bear, elk, wolf, coyote, and lynx. Smaller animals such as the raccoon, rabbits, and squirrel also provided meat. Both land and

77

Deer were plentiful and one of the chief sources of food for the Pomo Indians.

water fowl were very prevalent. All kinds of fresh and salt water fish were available for the taking.

Before the white man came, the Indians in this area spoke seventeen different dialects of five basic Indian languages.

These people lived in villages, which were independent of each other. Each village was a political unit and in this way resembled the tribal villages of the plains or eastern Indians. Government was handled by captains who acted more in an advisory capacity than one of absolute authority. Each group of people in the town, which usually meant an extended family, had their own captain who inherited his position from the female side of the family. From all of these family captains, the people in the town elected a head captain for the entire village. Older men who were captains eventually gave up their positions to younger men.

The people of a town possessed the sole hunting, fishing, and food gathering rights in the lands surrounding their village.

If a lot of sickness or bad luck occurred the residents of a village might move a mile or two in an attempt to get away from the evil force that they believed had overtaken their old village. If a village became crowded, some of the families would move a few miles away, but still considered that they belonged to the original village.

The old time community houses of the Pomo were usually circular and stood on top of the ground. These houses were built forty or fifty feet in diameter so that a number of families, that were related, could live together. Houses were made of long willow sticks thatched with straw.

To build the house, a framework of poles was planted in the ground on the outside of the house border, according to the shape and size desired. Then the tops of these poles were brought together in the center of the house and tied to a horizontal ridgepole. This framework was then covered with a thatch of long grass. A large circular opening was left in the center for light and for the smoke to escape. Each row of thatch was held in place by a horizontal pole

78

that in turn was covered by the next row of thatch. In this way a waterproof permanent house was built for the winter.

Each family had a small fire for its own cooking and its own private entrance as well. These individual families were allotted space around the edge of the circle. The center of the circular house was given over to community cooking such as making acorn mash, bread, and roasting meat. A larger fire was kindled there for this purpose.

The ceremonial and sweat-houses were similar in many ways. Both were circular and domed; both were excavated to a depth of three or four feet; both had a single doorway, a large center pole, and a fire between the center pole and the door. The roofs were supported by poles and covered with brush upon which dirt had been spread.

Ceremonial houses were very large. They were large enough to hold several hundred people. They had a diameter of about sixty or seventy feet. In addition to the doorway and smoke hole, they had small openings around the sides for ventilation. A hollow drum log was suspended over a hole in the floor by buckskin ropes that kept it from touching the ground. This made it possible to strike the drum when sitting on the ground. The drum position was at the back of the house.

The sweat-house was smaller and had room for only forty men. Women did not go into the sweat-houses. But the men went into the sweat-house twice a day, once in the morning and once in the evening. Each time a man went in he carried an armful of firewood for the fire. Since the heat was intense the men could not stand it very long. When they got too hot they ran outside to cool off before diving into the river.

In the summer, because of the heat, temporary brush structures were built along streams or in other shady places.

Pomo baskets were quite distinctive. They were very well made and ornamented with feathers and beads.

Pomo Medicine Man

The women tattooed their faces with three straight lines, one from the middle of the lower lip to the chin and the other two extending diagonally from each corner of the mouth.

The men smoked pipes made of ash. Wild tobacco was used and was carried around in a weasel-skin bag along with the pipe.

Dead persons were cremated, not buried. On death, persons were wrapped in their most valuable skins and wampum. Then the body was placed in a fire that had been set in a hole dug in the ground.

Bow and arrow, throwing stones, and snares were used in catching birds and animals. Small brush blinds were built near springs. The Indians hid behind them and when the animals came to drink they were shot with bow and arrow. Slings made of a small piece of buckskin and cord were used for throwing stones. Snares were used in catching birds, deer and other animals.

The acorn provided the chief vegetable food. These acorns were available from several varieties of oaks that were plentiful. All kinds of animals from the larger elk to small squirrels and gophers, as well as most varieties of birds, were used for food. A great variety of snares and traps were devised and used in their capture.

Sometimes, when food was scarce, toasted grasshoppers were eaten. To obtain them, grass fires were set in a circle and as the fire burned toward the center the grasshoppers could not get away. Their wings were singed and they dropped into the burning grass and were roasted. When the fire died down the Indians collected the grasshoppers and ate them.

In the early days the men sometimes wore blankets made of the skins of rabbits. The women wore robes of deerskin. The deerskins were tanned to make them soft but the hair was not removed. Neither men nor women used moccasins or hats. Belts made of either beads or feathers were worn for ceremonials and dances. Ear pendants carved from leg or wing bones of large birds were worn suspended from a hole in the lobe of the ear. In addition to being carved these bones were decorated on both ends with tufts of bright feathers.

A mourning ceremony took place during the burning. The person's ghost was said to remain on earth. After the burning was over the mother and sisters of the deceased rubbed the ashes of the burned body on their faces.

It was from these Pomo Indian villages that the early settlers captured children and adults alike and made slaves of them. The difference between slavery here and on the southern plantations was that in California a white family was likely to have only a slave or two who worked in the house or gardens while in the south, plantation owners would have a large number of negro slaves. Many people tried to justify the practice of captured Indian servants on the basis that the Indians were much better off under these conditions.

Pomo basket decorated with beads and feathers

YUROK

Approximately a hundred years ago the Yurok Indians were living in the Trinidad Bay area of California. This is in Northern California just a couple of hundred miles south of what is now the Oregon-California border.

The Yurok were a fine looking and intelligent tribe. They were strong and muscular individuals. Their skin was cinnamon color and their cheeks were pink. Like other North American Indians they had little beard as the chin hairs were plucked out. The men either burned their hair off about one inch long or wore it in long, stiff braids. The women wore their hair smoothly combed and unbraided. It was allowed to fall over the shoulders. Jewels were worn in their ears.

When five years old, little girls were tattooed with a black strip continuing from both corners of the mouth to the chin. Every five years another line was added to this one. On special occasions the men would paint their faces with designs by using a deep red-brown varnish.

During the summer men went naked. In the winter they wore shoulder wraps of tanned deerskin. The women wore aprons, front and back, that extended to the knees. In the summer these aprons were made of laced strips of deerskin. For winter use, they were made of fur or goose down.

Men always carried their bows and arrows with them. They were either held in hand ready for use or kept in a quiver, made of fox or beaver skin, that was slung over the shoulder. The bow, about three and one half feet long, was made of the root of the fir tree reinforced with a bear's sinew. Arrows were made of a combination of reeds and cedar wood. The base was provided with two rows of feathers. The tips were made either of volcanic glass, iron, or ivory. All were dangerous as they usually remained in the body that was shot. Other weapons included the ax, the club, the lance, and the javelin. Each Indian man also usually carried a knife that resembled a cutlass.

The homes of the Yurok were made of planks, usually of red-wood trees. These huts were about sixteen by twenty feet in diameter with walls four to six feet high, rising to ten or fifteen feet at the point of the roof. The door was an oval hole in one side about two feet wide. The occupants crawled in and out of this opening which was smeared with the blood of a sacrificed animal in order to ward off evil. A hole in the roof served as a flue for the fire and as a window. In bad weather, a cover was dropped over this opening.

A hole dug in the middle of the floor became the fireplace. The fire was never allowed to go out. The Yurok sat and slept around the fire. Older persons had the spots nearest the fire and the younger children sat at a greater distance from it. The huts and the surrounding courtyards were kept very clean.

The graveyard was located in a fenced spot in the center of the village.

At daybreak the Yurok Indians washed at the neighboring spring and dried themselves in the rays of the morning sun. Then the father opened the flue, stirred up the fire, and after assigning the daily work to members of his family, went hunting or gathered wood. The children hunted for acorns, roots, berries, and wild potatoes. When the tide was low the women would go to the seashore to look for shellfish and other sea foods. Food was not preserved but prepared when needed. Acorn meats were one of the main sources of food. These were made into a mush that was then smeared on the inside of a container. The mush was then baked by having hot rocks placed in the container. Oysters, mussels, and clams were also favorite foods.

The Yurok led a solitary, quiet family life. A young man could not marry until he was able to give his bride a string of rare shells as long as his arm, and a few red feathers. These then became the property of the first boy born so that he could use them in getting his bride. The father taught his sons to be hunters and the mother taught her daughters to be good housewives.

84

Yurok Indians searched and sorted shells. Dentalia shells were used as money by the Yurok.

Young children were taught respect for the superior beings, old age, and the chief. It was their religion to love their relations even after death. The hereafter was considered to be like this world, only better. The soul of one who was evil on this earth was supposed to be transmitted to an animal until he paid for his evil, then the soul went to the next world.

They worshiped the sun and moon as lesser divinities. Prayers were said to their divinities aloud while walking, running, or dancing. Evil spirits were believed to be in the air and showed themselves in storms.

The Yurok had a system of laws that was a standard by which they acted toward each other. Everyone was responsible for obeying all the laws. Every time a law was broken the individual breaking it had to make a payment of property such as food, hides or utensils, to the person that he hurt.

Dentalia shells were used as money by the Yoruk. The longer the shell the more valuable it was. Shells were strung on strings that were $27\frac{1}{2}$ inches long. When compared to American money a dentalia shell $1\frac{7}{8}$ inches long was worth twenty-five cents while one $2\frac{1}{2}$ inches long was worth five dollars.

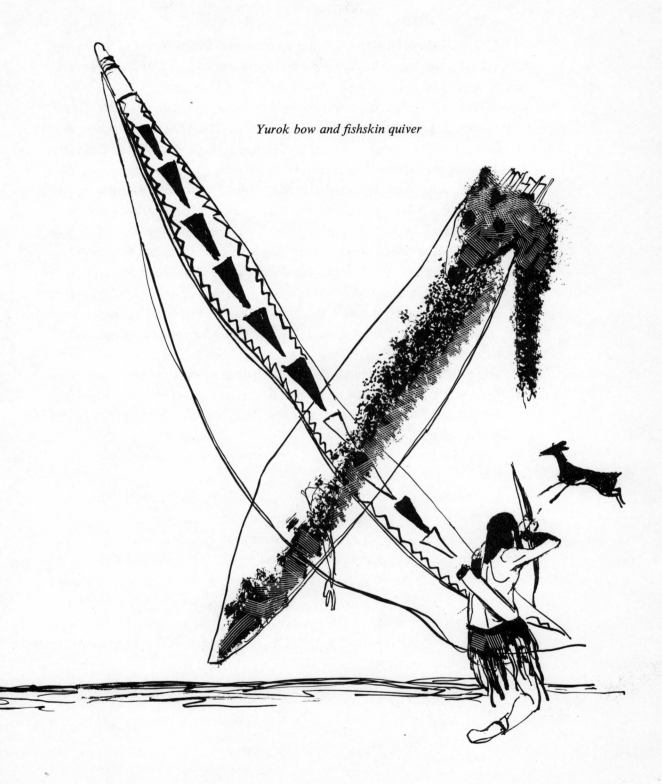

Yurok bow and fishskin quiver

VALLEY NISENAN

The Nisenan Indians are the Southern Maidu who occupied the Sacramento valley. They lived on the shores of the Sacramento and American Rivers.

Houses were earth covered, sometimes containing mats made of tule reeds to support the soil roof or to line the walls. Assembly houses and sweat-houses were made in the same way. Villages usually consisted of six or seven houses.

Rafts designed like boats were made of redwood planks. Boats were made from tule reeds by weaving. One-piece paddles were used for power.

A woman wore a bark or tule apron. In winter she wore a duck feather blanket, and a man wore a shawl of tule. The bark used for an apron was from the willow tree.

Short bows and arrows were used for hunting. The spear was used only in war although, in salmon fishing, a harpoon was sometimes used.

Clam shells were used as both spoons and knives. Bone and wood were cut and shaped with flat sharp stones.

An earth oven was used to cook tule roots, plants, and dried powdered salmon.

Acorns were knocked down from trees with sticks. People sometimes owned their own trees.

Spring salmon were caught on the American River. This was usually done by trapping them in weirs and then scooping them up in nets. Salmon was preserved by drying it raw, cooking and then drying it, or cooking, drying and then crushing it into powder.

Deer were hunted for meat, and salt was collected and used in seasoning.

Coarse, open-work willow baskets were made by the men to be used in carrying a variety of objects. Close-woven baskets were made by the women.

String and rope were made from a plant like the tule. The stems

88

The Kusku, or Big-Head cult, in central California danced to the spirits in pin-cushion headdresses with rods tipped with feathers or poppies. They carried a deer-head quiver and a bow or rattle.

were gathered in the fall, soaked, beaten, and the long fibers drawn out. Then the fibers were spun into string or rope. The rope was used for binding material. Fish and bird nets were made from the string. Nets were stretched over the water at night so that ducks and birds would fly into them.

Tobacco was the only crop that was planted. Seeds were saved from year to year. Pipes were made of wood and used chiefly by the old men.

Persons who died of a sickness were cremated and their bones buried. Those who were killed were buried without cremating. Small children were also buried without cremating. A bearskin and ornaments were put on a dead person so that he would not bother his living relatives. Weapons and personal effects of the dead were burned.

Shell spoon

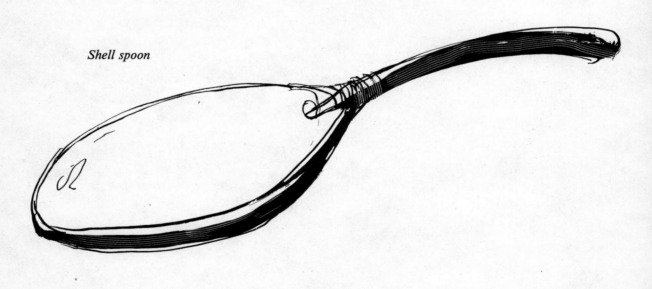

NORTHFORK MONO

The division of the Western Mono Indians, sometimes called the Monachi, that occupied the area of the northern San Joaquin River basin of California were known as the Northfork Mono. Sixty seven sites were inhabited by them in early American times.

These living sites were at small springs or small streams on the sunny slopes. At the bottom of the deep San Joaquin Canyon, the oaks provided inferior acorns so that these Indians preferred the higher elevations. However, they did maintain fishing camps down in these canyons.

A hut was built over a shallow excavation by erecting a conical framework of poles that were tied together at the top. These were then circled and held in place by grapevines. Then brush, bark, and grass were added as a covering. Earth was placed around the base and part way up to make the walls firmer. A hole was left in the roof for smoke. Ditches were dug to drain the water away from the hut. If a family moved any distance it was easier to just leave the hut standing and to build a new one. In case of death the hut was burned.

As a rule the population shifted from the valleys in the winter to the mountains in the summer, and then back to the valleys for the next winter. These camps ranged from one to eight huts with from one to thirty-nine people. Related families sometimes lived together in a camp. Each individual, in the course of a lifetime, lived in many camps.

These people traveled far and wide, and would sometimes be away from their houses for a year or more. They usually carried a supply of acorns along with them. With these the women prepared acorn mush at the various stops. Men hunted game on the way.

Acorns provided the major vegetable food, and deer, the major meat. Trout were often eaten with acorn mush. A large variety of seeds, bulbs, and greens were eaten. Nuts from the digger pine, sugar pine, and piñon were eaten and enjoyed very much.

When a hunter had killed a deer or other large animal he usually

Acorns provided
the major
vegetable food
for the Northfork
Mono as they did
for many California
tribes

shared it with others living at his camp. Strips of venison were often served with cold acorn mush for a meal. The mush would be scooped out of the basket with the fingers and then the fingers put in the mouth palm down so that the mush could be scraped off by the bottom teeth. Mush was cooked in tightly-woven baskets by putting in hot stones.

Cider was made by crushing manzanita berries and letting water drip through them. It was drunk fresh. To gather the berries, the ground was brushed clean with sticks, the berries were beaten off with sticks, and then swept into a basket.

Seeds were collected by beating them off the plants into a basket. They then were dried over a fire, crushed, and made into a thick soup.

Mortars and pestles were used in grinding acorns and seeds. Obsidian was used in making arrow heads and other kinds of cutting edges and points. Wooden bowls were cut from oak. Steatite, a kind of soapstone, was mined and made into dishes and cooking stones.

Basketry was one of the chief crafts. Mono baskets were finely woven and used for many purposes: cooking, winnowing grain, storage containers, and water bottles. Baskets were made watertight by coating them with acorn mush. Designs were woven into many of the baskets. This was done by selecting colored weaving materials such as fern roots.

Milkweed fiber was gathered and woven into string. This string in turn was made into nets or used as string for tying. Soaproot fibers were used to make brushes.

A man bought his wife from her father. The closer she had stayed to her home the more he had to pay for her. There were very few unmarried men in Mono Indian society. Most men lived with their wives' families all the time.

The Northfork Mono were divided into two groups called "moieties." One was the Turkey and the other the Eagle. In Mono, these were called *Wihu* and *Kwina*. When one person met another he would ask, "Hi pue puk?" which meant, "What is your pet?", and the other person would answer, "Wihu" or "Kwina" depending on his moiety.

A man, as well as a woman, belonged to his mother's moiety. Each moiety had its own chief. People could get married to anyone as long as they were not related. The moieties functioned in feasts, ceremonies, and games.

Showing typical basket hat used in rituals

CHUMASH

Southern California, along the Santa Barbara coast, was the home of the Indian tribe called the Chumash. These Indians had a good disposition, were liberal and were perhaps the most advanced of all the California tribes. They were friendly toward the Spanish when they set up the California missions and began farming.

Houses of the Chumash were large half-sphere communal houses that were neatly built with a door at both the east and west ends, and they were partitioned into rooms. There was a skylight in the roof. Beds were built up high on bedsteads of heavy sticks. One reed mat served as a mattress while four others served as curtains which formed the partitions of the bedroom.

The young children would sleep on little beds under the big family bed.

The women wore their hair in a flowing style sometimes decorated with shells. Their skirts, usually stained red, were also decorated with shells of all descriptions. For ornamentation, as well as protection, they covered their heads with woven trays or baskets.

This area of California was a fertile land of plenty. Seeds, roots, and fruits so prized by these Indians grew in abundance. Flour was made from the roots of plants. Cresses, celery, and amaranth were gathered and eaten during the rainy season. Bear cubs were captured, fattened, and then butchered as we now do with pigs.

From the sea, they were able to get crabs, whitefish, and sardines; and from the rivers, trout, spinebacks, and turtles. Fishhooks for catching the larger fish were made from shells. Sardines were caught in large baskets, into which bait had been thrown.

The Chumash made fine baskets and were skillful in woodcarving. They did inlaid work of mother-of-pearl on the edges of stone mortars and other utensils. The women wove baskets, trays, and jars. These were made with reeds or willows of different colors.

Perhaps the most outstanding example of their woodcraft skill was their planked canoe which the men built with flint tools. There were no big trees from which to build dugout canoes, so they split planks from driftwood. After the planks were smoothed, holes were drilled along the edges and the planks were sewn together with heavy fiber cords and then sealed with a kind of asphalt. These canoes were some 15 to 25 feet long and were painted and decorated with bright colors.

Chumash Indians were famous for their plank canoes

LUISENO MISSION INDIANS

At the time these Mission Indians were studied there were six bands: Rincon, La Jolla, Pauma, Mesa Grande, Agua Caliente (Warner Ranch) and San Luis Rey Mission.

In all of these settlements, the people lived in adobe houses. Many of the houses had brush roofs. Some had thatched-roofed porches in front. In addition, many families also had a workroom with willow walls, and a willow and brush covered shelter for summer use. The houses were not built near each other but scattered about. They were usually about one eighth to one fourth of a mile apart. They had a well or were near enough to a mountain stream so that they could get their water from it. Each house stood on a small cleared piece of land.

These Indians cultivated peaches and figs, which they dried on flat baskets placed on scaffolds. Tobacco also grew about the houses. Most of the families cultivated wheat and barley. The wheat was used by the Indians, but the barley was for the horses.

Grain was threshed by first spreading it on the ground around a post and then driving horses around and around over it. The grain was separated from the chaff by rotating it in flat baskets. The chaff was lighter and was blown off by the wind or brushed off by hand.

Stone mortars and metates were used for hammering and pulverizing the grain and, in some cases, acorns as well. Grain, to be stored, was kept in large upright cylindrical willow-work storehouses called "mus'-co-nish." These storehouses, about four feet in diameter and six feet high, were made by winding willow limbs with the leaves on, around and around in a close spiral and weaving in the ends.

Every family had a number of large homemade clay water bottles known as "ollas." These "ollas" were usually covered with a piece of cloth that was kept wet. The evaporation of the water on the outside kept the water inside cool. These homemade clay "ollas" were also used to cook in. An "olla" containing water, soup or stew was kept on the stove cooking all the time. Just about every family had a small iron stove. In the summer time they were kept outside but in the winter they were brought inside in order to provide some heat also.

In the late fall, all of the Indians went to Palomar Mountain to gather the acorns of the black oak. The meal made from these acorns was used in making both mush and soup. Fresh meat or preserved meat was usually added to the soup.

Baskets about the house contained grains and such fruits and vegetables as figs, peaches, red peppers, onions, and grapes. Baskets were used for almost every purpose imaginable. There were large bowl-shaped baskets with flat bottoms for holding grains, open-work baskets of about six quarts capacity for use in gathering acorns, cone-shaped baskets used as hats, circular flat baskets for winnowing grain, and various bowl-shaped baskets for general use. Most of the baskets were straw color with designs in yellow-brown or blue-black. Most of the baskets were made by coiling grass.

The Luisenos were rather large and good looking by our standards. They lived to be fairly old and looked strong and healthy. Most families had several children.

Exactly a year after the death of a Luiseno Indian a mourning "fiesta" was held. At this time friends and relatives of the deceased built a large fire. Into this fire they threw fine baskets and clothes in honor of the dead. These baskets usually were of the finest workmanship and had sacred designs woven into them.

Graves were marked with mounds a foot high with a fence around them. In addition, they had a low wooden cross on which had been hung a clock stopped at the hour of death. The deceased's name and date of death was cut or written on the crossbar. A lamp was placed on the other end of the grave. Whole and broken pieces of crockery such as cups, saucers, tumblers, tea pots, pitchers covered the rest of the grave.

These Indians loved fiestas and went great distances to take part in them. Dancing was the chief activity at a fiesta. Each person

98

*Dancing was the chief activity
at a fiesta of Mission Indians*

decorated himself for the occasion. The dancing costume was a kilt that hung down from the waist about fifteen inches below the hips. The men made their kilts out of feathers and the women made theirs out of shredded woven bark.

The young men loved rabbit hunts. They would choose up sides and see which side could club the most rabbits. Rabbits were chased on horseback and killed by throwing club-like sticks down on them. After the hunt was over the rabbits were roasted whole, without opening, in the hot ashes of a fire that had been prepared for that purpose.

Mission Indians threshed grain by spreading it on the ground around a post and driving horses around over it. The grain was separated from the chaff by rotating it in flat baskets until the chaff blew away.

A Hopi kachina doll was an image representing a clan spirit

Chapter IV **INDIANS OF THE SOUTHWEST**

THE **I**NDIANS of the Southwest occupied the area of what is now Arizona and New Mexico and adjacent parts of California, Utah, Colorado, Oklahoma, Texas and the northern parts of the states of Sonora and Chihuahua in old Mexico.

The climate of an area influences the lives of the people who live there. Indians living in this area had to develop means of dealing with extremes of temperature and with low rainfall. The need for water kept most of these people near the rivers. They built their villages in the valleys of the Gila, Colorado and Rio Grande rivers. To keep cool in the summers some of them went to the mountains.

It is believed that four different cultural groups lived in the Southwest before the white man came. These were called *Anasazi, Hohokam, Mogollon,* and *Patayan.*

The Anasazi lived in what is northeastern Arizona, northwestern New Mexico, and the adjacent areas of Utah and Colorado. These Anasazi people are believed to have first lived there about 400 A.D. — over 1500 years ago. They have been called *Basketmakers* because they made fine baskets. These baskets were so tightly woven together, they could hold water and carry heavy loads.

The Anasazi hunted with spears, clubs, and darts thrown with the aid of a throwing board. They also gathered wild fruits, vegetables, nuts, and berries.

Later on, the descendants of these Indians were called *Pueblos* by the Spanish and have had that name ever since. These Pueblo Indians continued to hunt and gather food and learned to do gardening before the white man came. They lived in villages built of stone masonry called *pueblos* from which they got their name.

The Hohokam are thought to have come to the southern Arizona region about the time of the birth of Christ, almost 2000 years ago. Some of the earliest of these people lived in caves. Later on they lived in pit-houses. They procured food by hunting, gathering plant products, and gardening. It is believed that the present-day Papago and Pima are descended from these early Hohokam.

The Mogollon occupied southwestern New Mexico and southeastern Arizona. They ceased to exist in this country about 1400. It is thought that they might have moved down into Mexico.

The Patayan occupied the area between present-day Prescott, Parker, and Needles, Arizona. There is little known about these early people. Perhaps they are the ancestors of the Yuman-speaking Indians of today.

Indians lived in the Southwest for more than 1500 years before any white men came. The first white men to see these Indians were the Spaniards who came north through Mexico. They were explorers, gold-seekers, missionaries, conquerors in suits of armor and were in the Southwest sixty-six years before the Pilgrims settled Plymouth.

Over a sixty year period many Spanish expeditions explored the area. They made extensive contacts with the Pueblo Indians of the Rio Grande Valley and in western New Mexico. Missionaries were left at all of the major Pueblo villages, however, most of these missionaries were killed.

Many Spanish-speaking white people settled in the Southwest. They wanted to use the Indians as forced laborers in the mines and on the ranches.

The Indians rebelled from forced labor many times between 1645–1680. By 1680 things were so bad that the Pueblo, Hopi and Apache Indians joined together to fight off the Spanish. The Indians were united under a Pueblo Indian from Taos, New Mexico, named Pope. Messengers were sent to all the tribes with knotted cords that indicated the day the rebellion was to take place. Someone tipped off

104

the Spaniards and so, to surprise them, the Indians had to start the rebellion two days earlier than they planned.

Hundreds of Spaniards were slain by the Indians who also destroyed all the written records of the Spaniards that they found and many of the churches and missions. Spaniards who escaped along with the Indians loyal to the Spaniards fled and planned how they could regain control.

The Spaniards regained control over the Indians twelve years later. The Indians rebelled again in 1696, but by 1700 the Spaniards ruled over all the Pueblo tribes of the Rio Grande. However, they never gained control over the Hopi in northern Arizona.

From 1687 to 1711 Father Kino established many missions in southern Arizona and northwest Mexico including the famous one of San Xavier known as *The Dove of the Desert* outside of Tucson, Arizona. Father Kino designed and directed the building of these missions. He also taught the Indians how to raise livestock and various plants.

When Mexico won its independence from Spain in 1821, the Indians rebelled again.

After the end of the war between the United States and Mexico, the government of the United States was not able to control the raiding Indians in the Southwest at once. Therefore, many of the Indian groups went on the warpath. The last major difficulty ended with the capture of Geronimo, the Apache chief, in 1888, not so many years ago.

Although the Spaniards did put many Indians in forced labor, they also helped them in many ways. It was the Spaniards who brought sheep and goats, which were secured by the Navaho who lived in the highlands of New Mexico, Utah, and Arizona. The Navaho and Apache stole or otherwise got Spanish horses that they later rode when they raided the Spanish and Indian villages. The Indians had corn from prehistoric times, but they got oats, wheat and barley from the Spaniards. They had wild grapes but obtained peaches from the Spaniards. The Spaniards also introduced the Indians to various garden vegetables such as beans, onions and beets.

Before the Spaniards came, the Indians had been using masonry walls, but the adobe-brick, corner fireplace and chimney were introduced by the newcomers.

Because garden tools, and other items of metal, were in such short supply, the Spaniards could not help out much this way. Therefore, the Indians had to continue to farm with a digging stick.

Pueblo men generally wore a breechclout for everyday, added a shirt during the winter, and a blanket and kilt when necessary. The Navaho men adopted the blouse and split trousers worn by the Spanish men. The Navaho women also used the breechclout but with a blanket dress and an additional blanket when necessary for warmth. The Spanish introduced a lacy garment over the blanket dress for women. The Indian women also took over the blouse and full skirt of the Spanish.

The Spanish had no influence on the substitution of pottery for the baskets of the Pueblos. The change had taken place before they arrived. Weaving had been done before the Spanish arrived, but they did make wool available to the Indians. Metal working was introduced by the Spanish and Mexicans about 1850.

Many different Indian tribes occupied the Southwest when white men first arrived. Indians of some of these tribes still live in the same places. The largest tribes of the Southwest were the Navaho, Hopi, Apache, Papago, Pima, and Mohave.

HOPI

The Hopi live in what is called the northern desert plateau, which averages about 5,500 feet above sea level in the northeastern part of Arizona. Very little rain but quite a bit of snow falls. The mesas are about 400 feet above the valley floor. Summer is marked with some rain and thunder, the fall and spring by being very dry and the winter with snow. Sage brush, yucca, creosote bush, and cactus grow on the plateaus and in the valleys. Piñon, juniper and western yellow pine grow on the mesas. Rabbits, coyotes, foxes and antelope inhabit the mesas. Deer and elk are found at higher elevations.

It is estimated that these same Indians were living here at the time of the discovery of America by Columbus in 1492, probably several hundred years earlier. In 1540, when Coronado, the Spanish explorer, entered the Southwest, the Hopi villages, with the exception of Oraibi were located in the valleys. It was just after the Pueblo rebellion of 1680 that the other villages moved to the top of the mesas for protection. Since there was very little soil and no water at the top of these mesas, living was most difficult.

Not only did the Hopi have to protect themselves from the Spanish, but from the Navaho, Ute, Paiute and Apache who raided them.

Today a number of villages have sprung up down in the valleys. Since it was no longer necessary to live on the mesas for protection some Indians now live in the valleys so as to be nearer water.

The United States government set up a reservation for the Hopi in 1882 and also established a school. A few years later the United States government started to divide up the land so that each Hopi family would receive 160 acres. The people of Oraibi, one of the oldest towns, refused to have anything to do with the plan and pulled up the surveyor's stakes. Our government sent in soldiers, and the Indians of Oraibi declared war on the United States. Five chiefs were taken prisoner by the soldiers. With their chiefs prisoners, the Hopi Indians gave up the war.

By 1904 some Indians grew more friendly to the white man. Very little rain fell for the next two years and in 1906 the Indians who were friendly with the whites, were blamed. Those friendly to the whites and those hostile to the whites agreed to settle their dispute by means of a pushing contest or a "push-a-war." In this "push-a-war" each side lined up and tried to push the other side over a line. The Friendlies won and the Hostiles left the village before nightfall. Since the Hopi do not believe in violence, they settle their arguments by this kind of war.

For a Hopi, the most important people are his relations. The woman is head of the Hopi family. It is the mother's clan who owns the springs and farms. Each child has a ceremonial parent besides his own parent. For a boy, it is a man; for a girl, a woman.

When a man gets married, he moves into his wife's household, that is, the home of her mother. The children belong to their mother's clan. The father still is a member of his mother's clan. A Hopi clan is composed of an elderly woman and all her female ancestors and descendants, plus all the males related by blood to these women. All control of the family is held by the mother. The mother's brother, with the help of the supernatural beings called Kachinas, is the one who makes the children behave, not the father or mother. A boy joins the ceremonial societies and kiva of his ceremonial father. Girls join a woman's society.

The Hopi believe that when a person dies he just changes his residence to the underworld. All Hopi want to get married for if they do not, they cannot go to the underworld.

The men conduct their religious ceremonies in buildings called kivas. Kivas are owned by a group of men who are charged with keeping certain ceremonies going. Kivas usually measure about 12 feet by 24 feet, and are constructed on the edge of a mesa, and are wholly or partially underground. Walls are built of stone masonry. The clan owns the ceremonies which are held in the kiva, but they are put on by the different fraternities. The most important part of

Hopi ceremonial corn dance.

the kiva is a hole in a board, sunk in the floor. This hole in the board is known as the *sipapu*. It is through the real sipapu, that this hole represents, that people go when they die to get to their place in the underworld where they continue their life.

Their chief god is Kokyang the Spider Woman, who is the center of everything and gave the Hopi all the skills that they have. Other gods include Masawu, who represents death and fire; Satugnangu who represents good; Kwantaga the god that guards the gate of the Sipapu to the underworld; Muinwu, the god of reproduction; Tawa the sun god who travels the sky every day and who has his kiva in the Pacific Ocean; and Mu-Yao the moon god who provides light at night. Kachinas are thought to include supernatural spirits and the spirits of ancestors, who in many cases bring rain.

Hopi Indians believe that the gods and Kachinas came up from the underworld with the regular people and that this place was the Grand Canyon. Then they wandered until they located their present villages.

Until they are six years old, all children are taught by their mothers. Before they are ten, both boys and girls are initiated into the Kachina cult. During this initiation they stand on a sand painting while they are whipped by the Kachinas. They later learn that the Kachinas are their own relatives and friends, but are sworn to keep it a secret from the younger children. The ceremonial fathers and mothers, much like our godparents, are appointed at this time. Before they are seventeen, girls go through a four-day corn-grinding rite. The boys between fifteen and twenty-five, and before they are married, join one of the ceremonial societies, at which time they spend four days in the kiva and are said to be reborn.

Old people have to train others to take their places in the ceremonials before they die. People are believed to die because of old age or because they have not lived right. Anyone with a good heart and an untroubled mind can sponsor a ceremonial. Hopi emphasize individual freedom, but feel they have to conform to the Hopi way.

110

Hopi snake dance

Every man devotes part of his time to religious ceremonies.

Since the Bear clan came up from the Grand Canyon first, the Bear clan head is village chief. This chief settles all arguments about land. His jurisdiction is limited to his village, for the Hopi are not a tribe but a group of individual villages and clans.

Today the Hopi face many problems. One is the change in their reservation boundaries. This has come about as their land quota has been cut by the government. Another is the grazing law that requires each family to cut down on the number of sheep that they raise. This is disturbing to the Hopi because importance and wealth are measured by the number of sheep a family owns. The building of a highway through their land has also brought problems. The Hopi formed a tribal council in accordance with the request of the United States government. However, since the more traditional Hopi warned against non-Hopi organizations, this has not been very successful.

PUEBLO INDIANS OF NEW MEXICO

Pueblo Indians of New Mexico settled near or on the various river banks, particularly the Rio Grande and its tributaries. The major Indian groups of the New Mexico pueblos being the Laguna, Zuni, Isleta, Acoma, Santo Domingo, Taos, Jemez, and San Ildefonso.

Although they were participants in the Pueblo rebellion of 1680, some of the Zuni were baptising their children as Christians some twenty five years later.

Prior to that time, native religious ceremonies were associated with houses at Zuni. The sacred chamber was the living room of the person offering the ceremony. Ceremonies were according to a complicated calendar and held three times a year.

Agriculture was a clan or household activity. Soil was prepared with a digging stick and by 1902 some irrigation ditches were used. Prior to that time, water was hauled from the river. They raised corn, melons, wheat, squash, beans, peaches, and each family had a kitchen garden. They tried to keep a year's supply of grain on hand. Salt was taken from a lake about 42 miles south of the pueblo. Navaho and Apache also used this same salt lake, but conflicts did not arise because all Indians considered salt to be sacred.

Their meat came from sheep, rabbit, and deer.

Houses were made of stone or adobe bricks laid up with mud mortar and they had flat roofs. The pueblo structures although usually two stories high, went from one to five. The people were divided into clans according to the mother's line.

The Zuni men during the period of the Indian rebellion wore shirts and pants that were really joined leggings. The women wore dresses and shawls. They also bought blankets to wear from the Navaho. Their baskets were bought from the Apache, and they used Mexican dollars in their silversmithing.

The people of Acoma were supposed to have come originally from Zia pueblo. They settled halfway between Albuquerque and Santa Fe, New Mexico. Spanish explorers discovered them in 1539

112

Pueblo structures were from one to five stories high. The golden eagle was sometimes captured and trained to hunt.

*Ruins of a pueblo show the kiva
which was partly underground*

at which time these Indians were very friendly. A mission was founded here in 1629, they revolted in 1680 and have been unfriendly since that time. They are very indifferent to white men and their ideas.

The houses of Acoma are of three-story construction. Very little furniture is used. They make their living farming and growing corn, alfalfa, chili and beans. Sheep are individually owned, but grazed on pueblo public land. Both pottery and wool are sold.

About 30 miles southwest of Santa Fe is located the pueblo of Santa Domingo. This is the most conservative of the pueblos and most of the people refuse to speak to outsiders at all. On ceremonial days all foreigners have to leave. This is the only pueblo that has not split on the use of modern ideas. These people also believe that they came from the middle of the earth.

They were flooded out a number of times and also had to flee from the Spanish.

They were a conservative people, opposed to change. Men let their hair grow long, wear old-time clothing and moccasins. These people are not supposed to leave the pueblo for more than a day without permission.

Their farm products include corn, squash, beans, grain, garden produce, sheep and goats. Pottery and jewelry are made for the tourist trade.

Everyone, including the women, belongs to one of two kivas. The secret and curing societies are very important. All ceremonies except the curing ones are held in the kivas. The curing ceremonies are held in private homes. Many sacred springs are located near the pueblo.

Another interesting pueblo of New Mexico is that of Jemez located in Sandoval County. This is the last group of people to speak Tewa. At one time, however, there were seven pueblos speaking this language. Eventually as the others died out, the remaining people moved to Jemez and brought with them all of their ceremonies.

The houses at this pueblo are made of adobe bricks which are made of clay and straw, and dried in the sun. They are built in rows or set apart in a grid pattern. The houses are owned by the men of the family rather than by the women as in the more westerly of the other pueblos. Outdoor ovens are used for baking bread. They are in Zuni and other pueblos.

The communal irrigation ditches provide the water for their gardens. They raise corn, wheat, beans, squash, chili, gourds, grapes and garden produce. All of the garden work is done by hand. Chickens are common and just about every family has a dog. Piñon nuts are collected and sold.

The men wear present-day American, or in some cases, older American clothes. Women wear a dress of black native-woven cloth over one shoulder. This is belted in at the waist. Moccasins are worn rather than shoes. Shawls and blankets, purchased at the stores, are also worn.

Between the ages of six and eight, boys are initiated into either the Eagle or Arrow Society. Ceremonial whipping is used as with the Hopi. Most men belong to one of the two clown societies. These societies are also open to women. The older men are the most active in ceremonies. Clown society members dance at the warriors' ceremonies.

These Indians are married in the Catholic Church. However, before the Catholic wedding they exchange gifts and have a corn-grinding ceremony. The church also provides for the burial services. In addition, the Arrow Society holds a ceremony and prayer sticks are deposited.

Two societies practice ceremonies that are supposed to cure ills, believed caused by witches. Persons do not have to join a curing society, but they do have to pay for a cure if someone gets sick and wants help. The Snake Society has a snake hunt and treats for snake bite.

The village of San Ildefonso is one of the most well-known pueblos. A myth, handed down by word of mouth, states that their ancestors came from Mesa Verde, an area of prehistoric structures in southwestern Colorado. Down through the years the population of San Ildefonso has been steadily decreasing.

In 1918, because of a dispute, the pueblo split in half. The nature of this dispute is not known to persons other than the Indians of this village. Since then, a great deal of discontent has developed. The spirit of cooperation is not as evident as it used to be.

Witchcraft is one of the major crimes at San Ildefonso. At the present time, persons believed to be witches are not usually punished, but at one time they were put to death.

Agriculture was once the basis of San Ildefonso economy. Many younger men now work on government projects. Both men and women work on pottery.

Another one of the better known pueblos is Taos. It is the most northerly pueblo on the Taos River. The people here speak Tiwa. Half of the town is on one side of the stream and half is on the other.

The houses are from one to five stories high and it is said that these are the first American apartment houses. The village has seven kivas, which are separate from the village houses, and partially under ground.

These people took part in the Indian Rebellion of 1680 and fought with the Americans in 1847 against the Spanish. At one time there was a strong stress on war, and enemy scalps were used in some of their ceremonies. This is one of the many resemblances to the plains Indians.

For years irrigation has been used to provide water for some garden crops, and wheat and corn. They have about five to ten head of cattle per family. Other animals raised include turkeys, pigs, horses, as well as dogs and cats. Sheep and goats are noticeably absent.

Years ago hunting was an important activity. Communal rabbit drives were common. Bears were also hunted.

Today they have very few crafts but a few people make some undecorated pottery, and do beadwork. Men basically use American dress except that the seat of the trousers is sometimes cut out to make leggings out of these trousers. Then a cotton blanket is worn over the head and around the body. This blanket comes down and overlaps the leggings. Many men also wear cowboy boots that have been modified by taking off the heels.

At birth every child is promised to a kiva, which is a house of worship. People tend to use the kivas on their side of the river. The training period usually lasts for about a year and a half. Boys are initiated between their eighth and tenth birthdays. Girls, as part of their ritual, spend four days in isolation. For the final initiation everyone goes to a place called Blue Lake. The ceremonies are put on by groups and not by the members of the kivas.

Curing of diseases is not done by societies, but by individual men or women curers called *shamans*.

Pueblo clown dancer

NAVAHO

It is often said that the Navaho, as well as some other Indians are in the American world but not of it. By this is meant that although these Indians live in America, they are quite different than the rest of the people who live here. The present Navaho reservation is the northeast corner of Arizona, southeastern Utah, and northwest New Mexico. A large section in the center of the Arizona portion is the Hopi Indian Reservation.

Some people believe that the Athabascan-speaking people, of which the Navaho are part, arrived in the southwest about one thousand years ago. It is believed that these people might have come from northwestern North America. This might be true, for the Navaho speak a language similar to Indians of the northwest. The Navaho were impressed by the settled life and ceremonials of the pueblo Indians and in many cases imitated them.

Even after the Indian Rebellion of 1680, the Navaho did some raiding but only for what they needed. They never organized for war. The Navahos and other southwest Indians stayed clear of the plains Indians who had war organizations.

When troops were withdrawn from the Indian territory of the Southwest during the Civil War, many Indians thought that they had defeated the white man and raiding went wild. General Carleton of the United States Army instructed the famous Kit Carson to take the New Mexico Volunteers and round up the Navahos. To avoid being put into camps, some of the Navaho Indians fled before Kit Carson's forces and went into exile and holed up in Canyon De Chelly and other canyons of northern Arizona and southern Utah. Finally, between six to eight thousand Navaho were captured and collected at Fort Wingate, Arizona. Later they were removed to the six thousand acre encampment of Bosque, Redondo, known also as Fort Sumner, New Mexico. As the Navahos were being hunted, all their fields and orchards were destroyed by the soldiers.

At Fort Sumner the Navaho could not build hogans, the kind

of houses they were used to, because of lack of wood and therefore they had to live in holes in the ground with roofs made of anything that they could find. General Carleton tried to get the Navaho to build adobe homes and to farm, but without much success. He did get a few irrigation ditches dug and some crops planted. However, the grasshoppers ate up everything that grew.

To feed the Navaho, the government had beef driven up from Texas, but these animals lost weight on the way. Then beef and flour were shipped in by the barrel, but it spoiled before it arrived. Food was very scarce.

There was no way to take care of the sick as the Navaho did not have their ceremonies and curing materials with them, and white doctors were not present. They begged to go back to their homeland after being reduced in numbers by starvation and sickness. They were finally allowed to return after the "Treaty Between the United States of America and the Navaho Tribe of Indians" was drawn up. This treaty provided, among other things, that both parties would stop fighting and keep the peace, the Indians would stay on the reservation and each Navaho family would be given one hundred and sixty acres to farm.

On returning to the reservation, they were encouraged to increase their herds of sheep and goats. This was done to make the Navaho self-supporting. Eventually some Navahos had large herds and a person became important if he had a lot of animals. Since the land could not support this many animals, the Indian Bureau tried to have the herds cut down. It was difficult for the Indians to understand why they should now cut down when they had just been encouraged to raise more.

In addition to raising sheep, goats and cattle, many Navahos now carry on small-scale gardening. To provide water, ditch irrigation is used in many places. Wild plant products that were once available no longer can be collected because they are eaten by the domestic animals.

120

A Navaho curing ceremony had the patient sitting on a sand painting while his illness was driven away with rattles.

Many Navahos make their living cutting lumber and gathering piñon nuts. In recent years the largest employer of Navahos was the railroads. Tribal enterprises include arts and crafts guilds, sawmill and wood products industry, motels at Shiprock and Window Rock, and a coal mine.

The Navaho generally traded at the nearest trading post. Although now many have cars and trade at Shiprock, Gallup, Winslow, and Holbrook. The trader in charge usually also ran the post office and handled local employment for the railroads. Trading was usually a credit proposition. That is, the trader lets the various Indians have material on credit and holds the checks they receive in payment. The trader formerly was everything to the Navaho. He read and wrote letters for him as well as posted information about tribal government regulations.

There is no such a thing as a pure Navaho. Down through the years they have married whites and Mexicans. The Navaho is willing to include anyone in his group. New clans are sometimes started to take care of new members.

Navahos like to have a good time and play practical jokes on friends. They like to sing and practice songs as they work. Later on, they will sing these songs at their ceremonials. Ceremonials are used for a good time as well as for religious purposes.

The mother is the head of the family, but the father represents it in public and ceremonial affairs. A man respects his mother-in-law by not looking at her or getting near her. To be sure that they avoid each other, the mother-in-law may wear a pair of small silver bells that ring as she walks around. The same is true for a woman and her father-in-law. Children receive their training from one of their uncles, that is, their mother's brother. He is the one that tells them what to do and punishes them when they are bad. Mothers and fathers seldom scold or whip their children, as they want them to love them.

Navahos live in clusters of hogans and make up what is known as an extended family. All the children belong to their mother's clan.

The father keeps membership in his mother's clan. When children marry, it must be someone not a member of either of the clans of their Mother and Father.

Navaho woman weaving a rug in the sunshine outside her hogan

YUMAN SPEAKING INDIANS

The Yuman speaking Indians include the Cocopa south of the city of Yuma; Yuma near the city of Yuma; Maricopa near the city of Sacaton; Mohave, near Parker; Walapai, Havasupai and Yavapai in the northern part of Arizona.

Those who lived in the river valleys stayed there most of the time. These people depended more upon farming than hunting. After the Spanish conquest, they raised garden vegetables and grain. They also gathered cactus roots for food.

The Yuma and Mohave would join together to fight the Maricopa. Special places were set aside as battle grounds. They would gather here and insult one another. Then one or more men from each group would be selected to fight. The battle continued until someone started to bleed. Then the war was over.

Religious experiences could be had through the medicine man or directly with the superior being on an individual basis. Contact was made through dreams and songs.

Those Indians living along the river banks cut rectangular platforms in the west bank of the river as the basis for their houses. Not much was done in the way of arts and crafts. They wove some cotton cloth and made pottery.

When the Yuma and Mohave joined to fight the Maricopa, one man was chosen from each group to fight. The battle was over when one fighter started to bleed.

*Apache
ceremonial
dancer*

APACHE

The name "Apache" came into use after 1600. In Zuni, it means *enemy people*. They earned the name because of the raids that they made on the other tribes. To protect themselves, they always hid their camps very well. Today they live on reservations in southern Arizona and New Mexico. These groups are known as the Western and Eastern Apache. Families of one group of Apaches, the White Mountain, used to visit the families of the Zuni. On occasion, other Apache groups visited and traded with other Pueblo Indians.

Up to one hundred years ago most of the Western Apaches hunted and gathered for a living. They gathered and used plant products, such as cactus fruits, mescal, mesquite bean pods, yucca fruit, piñon nuts, walnuts, acorns and berries of all sorts. Some planted crops in the valleys. They left their headquarters located in the valleys in the spring and roamed the mountain side, hunting as they went. In the fall they returned to their permanent homes in the valleys.

Eastern Apaches went out into the plains to hunt bison, but hurried right back so as not to be caught by the plains Indians.

Their homes were called *wickiups* and made of interlocking branches covered with bear grass. In the summer they lived under a thatched roof mounted on four poles called a *ramada*.

Clothing of 200 years ago was probably of buckskin. One hundred years ago it was anything that they could get from raiding. Today the Apache use American-type clothing.

Basketry is the oldest Apache craft. Their designs were excellent and were done in black or tan. The eastern group also made pottery. About a hundred years ago they started beadwork, but today very little craft work is done.

Religious activities are under the direction of medicine men who become very influential people. There is no ceremonial calendar and ceremonies are put on by medicine men when needed. The eastern Apache have dropped many of their old ceremonials.

127

The western Apache still have three major ceremonies known as the girls coming-out ceremony, the lightning ceremony, and the crown-dance ceremony.

When girls become women, they participate in a ceremony that runs for three or four days and nights. Sometimes this is held in connection with the Fourth of July. For the girls this is an endurance contest, for during the day they cook and do other work and then dance all night. The girls' families distribute gifts to the people in attendance.

If it is believed that lightning has struck a person, the lightning ceremony is held. This consists of songs and orations by the medicine man.

A group known as the Crown Dancers put on a series of songs alternating with dances in an effort to cure sick people.

Apache means "enemy people", a name given them by the tribes they raided. After the Apache secured horses they could strike and get away quickly.

PAPAGO AND PIMA

Papago means *bean eater* or *people who eat beans*. These people and their neighbors, the Pima, live in the southern, or desert area of Arizona. This is known as basin and range country. It consists of low desert mountains with valleys in between them. The washes, which are rivers that only run for part of the year, carry great quantities of water in the rainy season.

It is believed that both of these people are descendants of the Hohokam, mentioned earlier in this chapter. The dialects spoken by Papago and Pima are very closely related. By looking at them it is difficult to tell a Papago and Pima apart.

Before they were put on reservations, the Papago and Pima hunted animals, gathered plant products and farmed. Plant products used included cactus fruit, grass seeds, and mesquite bean pods.

Farming was done by planting before the summer floods which watered the newly planted seeds. This is known as flash-flood farming.

In the winter months they lived in the mountains near springs for water and trees for fuel. Hunting of deer and other animals was done at this time.

When late spring came the Papago would move across country toward the valleys. In the early summer they moved to groves of giant saguaro cactus to collect and process the fruit of that cactus. By boiling the juice of this fruit it could be made into jam and wine. The seeds were separated out and ground into flour.

In mid-summer they would leave for the valleys. When they arrived, ground would be cleared and seeds put in before the late summer rains arrived. They would stay at these farms until the water supply ran out. A few would stay to watch the crops. The rest would go back to their winter villages. In the fall they would return to harvest and transport the crops to the winter villages.

The Pima did not move about as the Papago did, but used irrigation water from the Gila River and stayed primarily in one place.

Before the Apache started their intensive raids in 1700, the

*Both Papago and Pima made
baskets to hold grain and
even liquids*

Papago had many separate villages and fields. In raiding, the Apache struck before dawn, got what they wanted and then vanished. For protection, the Papago had to concentrate in a few locations. Then in 1800 when the raids let up they again formed many smaller units.

Winter houses were made by using mesquite posts as a main framework. Then dried ocatillo and saguaro stalks were placed in between them. Mud was then plastered on both inside and outside. Summer homes were *ramadas*, roofs on four posts, like those used by the Navaho. Today, most of the new buildings are made of adobe brick.

Both Papago and Pima knew how to make baskets and pottery. Tightly woven baskets were used for liquids. Pots were made by the coiled method. They had a red design on a buff colored surface. A coarse clay was used in the making of water jars.

The individual villages were the important governing units and each of them operated independent of the others. They worked together only in emergencies, such as combating the raids of the Apache. After a man became thirty years old, he was allowed to vote. Council meetings were held every night. The head man had charge of all important objects such as scalps which were usually Apache.

The medicine men were in charge of religious activities. Individuals could acquire religious power through dreams. Religious power could also be gained by participating in an expedition to get salt at the Gulf of Lower California. Persons having this power could be dangerous to themselves and others.

Today, the men wear cowboy clothes such as a work shirt, trousers, shoes and a five or ten-gallon hat or a straw hat. Women thirty years and older tend to wear the Mother Hubbard one-piece dress made out of printed cotton material. Younger women wear modern clothing.

Today, some Papago still use flash-flood farming, some raise cattle, but most of them work for wages in the cotton fields.

132

Pima Indians farmed, gathered plant products and hunted, but stayed pretty much in one place.

Chapter V
INDIANS OF THE PLAINS

THE LARGEST Indian cultural area of North America is known as the Plains. It extends from the Mississippi River Valley on the east to the Rocky Mountains on the west, and from about the middle of Canada in the north to the lower part of the United States in the south. The plains country is characterized by its short-grass vegetation and dark-colored soil. It is miles of open, rolling country without many trees.

Because of the size of the territory, great fluctuations of both rainfall and temperature will be found from one place to another. This fluctuation of rainfall and temperature is also true for the same place from year to year.

Although the many Indian tribes of the plains had their own individual languages and dialects, all of these belonged to only six different basic language families. Each tribal language or dialect was related to one of these six language families. Members of tribes speaking different dialects of the same language could understand each other.

When tribes spoke different basic languages the only way that they could communicate with each other was by means of a sign language that most of them could understand. Various gestures meant different things. For instance a "chief" was represented by raising the index finger, pointing it vertically upward, then reversing the finger and bringing it down. For "rain" the gesture was to hold the hands at shoulder level, the fingers hanging down, and then push downward. "Cold" was indicated by clenching both hands and crossing the forearms in front of the chest with a trembling motion.

134

The eastern plains people became large-game hunters who depended on buffalo for food and clothing. Those of the basin and plateau tribes of the west used small game such as rabbits.

The eastern plains people were nomads. They lived in tipis. Dogs were used as pack animals. When the Spanish brought horses into the Southwest, some of them escaped to the plains where they multiplied until there were many wild herds. One hundred years later the Indians were using these horses to hunt buffaloes and move themselves and their possessions. Hides and skins were used for dress.

More often than not these tribes were warlike. Ceremonials were extensive and culminated in the sun dance.

In contrast, the basin and plateau tribes of the west were less warlike, had fewer ceremonials, and were not horsemen.

The sun dance was the most important religious festival of about twenty of the plains tribes. The festival was elaborate among the Arapaho, Cheyenne, and Dakota. Other of the plains tribes used selected portions of it. The Department of Interior prohibited the performing of this dance in 1904, but in 1935 changed its mind and removed the ban. After its reactivation, modern conditions caused some modifications of the ceremony.

As a rule, the dance was performed in the late spring or early summer when the bands of a given tribe reassembled after being separated for the winter. For many tribes the sun dance was a yearly affair.

The dance was usually performed as a result of a tribesman's vowing to have it held to relieve him of his worries. However, the reasons did vary from tribe to tribe.

The name "sun dance" is misleading as the dance does not center around the sun as a deity. Rather it is a combination of a number of important religious rites.

The dance is started by an Indian priest acquainted with the ritual who instructs the person pledging the dance. A pole with a fork is raised in the air with a bundle of brush, buffalo hide and offerings in the fork. The pole is said to represent an enemy, and the bundle an eagle's or thunderbird's nest. This pole serves as the center of a tipi frame that is then constructed. Buffalo skulls are used as an altar.

The Cheyenne dance pledger and his associates would fast for several days. At the same time they would gaze at the top of the central pole as they danced and prayed for power. The Crow pledger would stare at a sacred doll.

Sometimes the participants would torture themselves by threading skewers through the skin of their breasts or backs and then attaching ropes between the skewers and the central pole. Then the dancers danced and strained against the ropes until they tore themselves loose.

In addition to being a religious ceremony, the dance also served as entertainment for the spectators.

When the average person hears about Indians he immediately thinks about the roaming buffalo-hunting warrior Indian of the plains, wearing beaded buckskin and arrayed in a headdress of feathers, raiding on horseback or engaging in the sun dance.

No primitive group has captured the interest of Americans and Europaens as have the Indians of the plains.

The mounted, warring, roaming Indians who became so famous were not the original plains Indians nor the Indians that we know today. From about 1740 to 1800, as they were able to secure horses by theft and trade, their way of life changed. It must be remembered that horses were not available in North America until brought in by the Spanish and other European settlers. The great historical Indian period was from 1800 to 1870 with the famous Indian battles from 1850 to 1870.

Before the advent of the horse the plains Indians could not travel widely and successfully hunt very large animals. They had to rely on small game and garden produce such as maize, beans and squash.

136

Sometimes sun dance participants tortured themselves by threading skewers through their skin. They believed that they gained wisdom and power by dancing until they tore themselves loose.

CHEYENNE

The Cheyenne Indians, like many others of the plains, turned from gardening to mounted hunting as they were able to get horses. Because of their central location they became middlemen in the trading of horses and European trade goods from east to west.

On the first contact with white men, the French explorers, the Cheyenne were living in the upper Mississippi River Valley at a place that is now the Wisconsin-Minnesota border. These French explorers called this tribe of Indians *Cheyenne* which came from the Sioux word *sha hi'ye* meaning *speakers of an unintelligible language* for the Sioux could not understand the Cheyenne when they spoke. The Cheyenne call themselves *tsis tsis'tas* which means *people*.

Due to the rivalry between the French and English and the warfare in Wisconsin, Minnesota, and Illinois in the late 1600s the Cheyenne moved to the Dakotas and were settled near the Cheyenne River by 1700.

By 1800, life of the Cheyenne Indians had been influenced in many ways by the white man besides the introduction of the horse. Trade goods and especially guns had become available. Horses, buffalo hides, and furs could be traded for axes, knives, kettles, beads and the all-important gun. Horses were secured by raiding and trading. The buffalo hides and furs were obtained by hunting. Guns required lead and powder which meant horses and hides were always needed for trading. This caused the Cheyenne to step up their horse-raiding parties and buffalo hunting.

Guns gave a big advantage in warfare and raiding. For about one hundred years the plains became an arena of intense tribal conflict. Tribes that were first to get horses and then guns kept the whole area in turmoil.

Since subsistence depended primarily on the buffalo, hunting was regulated. Individual Indians were not allowed to hunt them on their own but had to hunt as a group in order to obtain enough

138

meat for the entire tribe. By hunting in groups the Cheyenne could circle a group of buffalo and pick off those that wandered away from the center of the herd. Since they were mounted on horses the Indians could ride up close and shoot them with bow and arrow. Even after they had guns, the bow and arrow was used because it could be loaded faster than the flintlock gun. Wounded buffaloes were killed with knives or spears.

After the animals were killed they had to be skinned, cleaned, cut up, and carried back to camp. This sometimes took days. Back at camp the meat was cut into strips, dried, smoked and made into "jerky" or pemmican, which kept very well. "Jerky" is the English term for the Spanish *charqui* meaning *dried meat*. Pemmican was made by pounding the dried meat together with fat. Sometimes berries, or other fruit were added. It was then stored in large skin sacks until needed.

Men and women each had specific work that they did. In no case did they do work belonging to the other sex. The work of the women consisted of all activities considered "domestic." These tasks included making the "jerky" or pemmican as well as the dressing of skins.

Men spent their time hunting and raiding. Wild sheep, deer, and antelope roamed the hills and were very plentiful. In addition to obtaining horses by trading and raiding, they also added to their herds by catching wild horses.

Horses were highly prized and a man's importance was measured by the number of horses that he had. The best horses were saved for hunting, raiding, and warfare. The others, along with mules, were used for the transportation of meat and household goods. These items were either tied on to the back of animals or placed on a travois. A travois was made of two poles strapped to the animal's back with the opposite end of each pole dragging on the ground. Travoises of different sizes were used on horses, mules, and dogs.

Skins, bones, and horn provided the basic materials for Cheyenne tools, homes, and clothing. These came from the buffalo, antelope, and deer. Bows were made of layers of horn backed with sinew; containers were of rawhide and horn; and drills, scrapers, and awls were made from antlers.

All Cheyenne clothing was made of skins. The skins of deer or antelope were preferred.

Women wore one-piece dresses that had open capelike half-sleeves. These dresses nearly reached to the feet. They were fringed and decorated with porcupine quills and beads. Women also wore leggings from the knee to the ankle and soft moccasins soled with stiff rawhide. In winter, a buffalo robe was worn with the hair-side in.

Men wore only a breechclout and moccasins in summer. In winter they wore fringed leggings and a shirt that overlapped the leggings. These shirts had full-length sleeves and some were ornamented with beads and fringed along the seams with the scalp locks of enemies. When they were decorated with the scalps they were called "war shirts" and worn only on special occasions.

Men paid particular attention to their hair and allowed it to grow as long as possible. Both men and women very often braided their hair on the sides.

The Cheyenne tribe was divided into ten bands, each with its own ceremonies and medicine. Persons could not marry within the same band because of the possibility of being related.

Except during the summer, the bands split up into family groups that traveled and hunted together. In the summer all of the ten bands of the tribe met for hunting and the performance of important tribal ceremonies. Each of the bands always camped in a particular place in relation to the other bands.

Within the tribe there were six military societies that accepted only the strongest, and most fearless men. Members of these societies also acted as policemen during the summer reunion, and on the organized hunts.

All affairs of the tribe were handled by a council of forty-four

140

It was common practice among the plains Indians to do a buffalo dance before a big hunt to secure its success. Buffalo meant food, shelter, tools and ornaments.

chiefs. Four of these were from each band and four from the tribe at large. All members of the council served for ten years. The council had to handle disputes and feuds.

Most Cheyenne men were considered great warriors. A young man grew important by capturing horses and keeping the enemy away by constant raids. Such a young man would show that he was generous by giving away the horses that he captured. Raiding parties would go out on foot and ride home the horses they acquired.

War parties were quite different from raiding parties.

A party of warriors would ride up and ambush the enemy. In raiding, the purpose was to secure horses, but war parties had as their aim the killing of the enemy. War parties were usually organized for revenge.

Cheyenne woman on a horse with a travois

CROW

The Crow of the western plains also is typical of the Indian of fiction. They occupied over 100,000 square miles in Wyoming and Montana until they were placed on a reservation. This area had mountains, valleys, prairies, and plains with water provided by mountain streams. This is the spectacular country which now includes Yellowstone National Park. Before the white man came, game such as buffalo, mountain sheep, grizzly bears, deer, elk, antelope, and waterfowl were found in abundance. Edible plants and berry-bearing bushes grew in profusion.

The Crow had a light reddish-brown color. He was tall, had straight black hair, and a prominent nose. Both the men and women were very strong.

They called themselves *Apsaroke* from which we eventually got the word Crow. The use of smoke signals and sign language made it possible for them to exchange ideas with other Indians that did not speak their language.

Like other Plains Indians the only domesticated animal that they had, until they got the horse from the white man, was the dog. The dog was used as a pack animal through the use of a travois. As members of the tribe acquired the horse in about 1650 they were able to move about more freely.

The only gardening done by the Crow was to raise a little tobacco for ceremonial purposes. Very little use was made of the fish that were so plentiful in the rivers as they were generally considered taboo. They lived mostly on big game. However, the women and girls did gather wild fruit, berries, edible plants and wild roots to supplement the meat diet.

During the winter they passed the time away in a protected spot near the bank of a stream. In the summer they moved frequently following the buffalo and other animal herds.

The principal weapon was the bow and arrow. The Crow carried their arrows in a skin quiver for protection. Ten good arrows were equivalent to a horse. The bow was of horn or wood and about three feet long. The arrows were made of a wooden shaft with feathers on one end and a point of bone, horn, or chipped flint on the other.

Large animals such as buffalo, antelope, deer and elk were usually killed in community animal hunts by driving them over cliffs or bunching them in a circle and then killing them off as was done by the Cheyenne. The meat might have been either roasted, broiled, or boiled. Meat was also preserved by being made into jerky or pemmican.

The most popular shelter was the tipi. A Crow tipi would be about 25 feet high and provide room for about 20 people. The main frame was made of four very large poles meeting at the top. About 20 other poles, arranged in a circle, leaned on the four main poles. Over this was stretched a cover of buffalo skins. Stones or pegs kept the cover on the ground. A hole with an adjustable flap was left at the top for smoke to escape. Sometimes painted or quill decorations were added. Soft skins or furs were placed on the ground for sitting and sleeping.

The Crow clothed themselves in skins from mountain sheep, antelope, deer, elk, and buffalo. Hides were made soft by treating them with buffalo brains and by scraping and rubbing. Children wore very little clothing. In the summer the men wore only the breechclout and moccasins. However, in the winter they added leggings, a long shirt, and a buffalo robe. The women wore moccasins, leggings, a sleeveless dress extending down to the feet and, in the winter, a buffalo robe.

Everyone took a bath in the river every day of the year. Great attention was paid to the care of the hair, especially among the men. It was oiled, perfumed and rubbed before being braided.

The men did the hunting, fighting and made the necessary weapons. Women gathered firewood, fruits, berries, and roots. They did all of the cooking. The women prepared skins and made the

144

Many Indians of the plains turned from farming to hunting buffalo as they were able to secure horses and follow the herds.

Decorated buffalo robe

clothing. This they embroidered with quills. The women also made, put up, and took down the tipis.

Thirteen clans, each with its own chief, made up the Crow tribe. Clansmen camped, worked, and feasted together. A man belonged to his mother's clan, not his father's clan. When a man died his property went to his brothers and sisters because they were of the same clan.

Because it was fairly easy to get enough to eat, the Crow Indians found plenty of time for games and sports. They spun tops, slid on the ice, coasted on toboggans, ran foot races, had archery contests, threw darts, and played dice. They were very fond of gambling.

Before a plains Indian had a horse,
he would hunt the buffalo by creeping
up on it in a wolfskin

COMANCHE

The Comanche Indians were one of the great tribes of the American West. For one hundred and fifty years they controlled the plains and prairies south of the Arkansas River, east of the Pecos River. This territory included what is now the adjacent sections of New Mexico, Colorado, Kansas, Oklahoma, and Texas.

Their superior horsemanship and fighting prowess made it possible for them to guard this land that they claimed. The name Comanche came to be associated with wildness, fierceness, and savagery. They were able to stop the advance of the French, Spanish, and Americans from the East for fifty years.

For the one hundred and fifty years that they controlled the southern plains they dominated all the other Indian tribes in the area. They fought and beat at one time or another the Ute, Pawnee, Osage, Tonkawa, Apache, and Navaho. These and other Indian tribes were within raiding distance and the Comanche took advantage of this.

The word *Comanche* comes from the Ute and means *enemy*. The original word was *Komantcia* which meant *anyone who wants to fight me all the time*. The Spanish picked this word up from the Utes and then the Americans got it from the Spanish.

In the sign language of the plains, the Comanche were known as the Snakes. The sign is to place the right hand palm down, with forearm across the front of the body, and then to move the arm to the right with a wiggling motion.

The Comanche country was generally level and cut through by a number of rivers. Plum bushes and grape vines grew along the streams. In the eastern section pecans, walnuts, and persimmons were also found. During the summer much of this area looked like a desert. But after the spring and summer rains, grass grew rapidly. In this warm climate, with its abundance of plant products and wild animals, food, clothing and shelter were relatively easy to obtain.

Operating as independent bands the Comanche kept on the move.

148

*The horse changed the Comanche way of life
as it did that of other Indians of the plains.
Horses became a symbol of prestige and wealth.*

However, campsites were carefully selected so as to provide food, shelter, safety, convenience, and feed for the horses. Within the camp there was no special plan except that all lodges were grouped around the lodge of the chief.

The women did the daily work of preparing the food, tanning hides, making tipis, and making clothes. The men spent their time discussing important subjects, raiding, hunting, making weapons, and amusing themselves. Children assisted their mothers or spent their time at play.

The Comanche men were of medium stature with copper-colored skin. The hair was never cut but worn long and ornamented on special occasions with silver and beads. The women were somewhat lighter. They aged prematurely, probably because of their hard lives.

The Comanche spoke a dialect of the Uto-Aztekan language known as *Shoshonean*. This is the same language spoken by the Shoshones who were closely related to the Comanche.

The Comanche were organized in family units and bands. Although each band had its own territory, other bands could use it when they cared to. Comanche bands never fought each other, but often joined together to make war on bands of other tribes. Persons generally married within their own band. Any time that they chose, persons could move from one band to another.

In large bands relatives usually camped near each other. One of the family head men was the head chief of the band and the other men became his advisory council.

Sometimes one band had a different way of doing things than another. For example, one band would make clothing out of antelope skins and another band preferred deer skins; one would make pemmican with berries and another made it without berries.

At one time there may have been as many as thirteen different bands. Six of these were outstanding and well known. The largest were the *Honey-Eaters,* (sometimes also called the *Hospitable,*) *No Meat, Steep Climbers, Raiders, Timber People,* and *Wasps.*

It was this last band that helped the United States Government in its war against the other Comanche. To this day other bands still dislike the Wasps.

It was the use of the horse, the buffalo, and the tipi that made the Comanche typical plains Indians. The horse changed the Comanche way of life as it did that of all of the other plains Indians. By using the horse, camps could be moved more easily. Buffalo could be hunted better on horseback than on foot. When food was scarce the horse could even be eaten. In addition, the horse made raiding possible. Hit and run raids could be made into the enemy's territory and the plunder carried out quickly and easily on horseback. Thus, both other Indian tribes and white settlements were attacked and plundered with the help of the horse.

It can be seen that horses were an Indian's most important property and determined his prestige and wealth. The Comanche obtained their horses by gift, trade, breeding, capturing wild ones, and by raiding. They got their first horses sometime after 1600 and had them in large numbers by 1650. One band was reported to have had 6,000 head. A Comanche named *A Big Fall By Tipping* was said to have owned 1,500 horses.

Wild horses were captured by driving them into pens, shooting them in the neck so as to stun them, or by lassoing them. Stealing horses was much better for an Indian than capturing them, for a brave could become highly respected for stealing them from his enemies. Among the Comanche, horses were private property. And the Comanche were the best horsemen known. One of the first things a young boy or girl was taught, was to ride.

The buffalo was also important to the Comanche. It provided clothing, food, and shelter. The Indians ate its flesh, the marrow of its bones, and even the contents of its gall bladder on raw liver. Of the edible parts, only the heart was not eaten. It was left for the magical increasing of the herd. A thirsty Comanche would drink the blood of the buffalo when water was not available. The buffalo hide

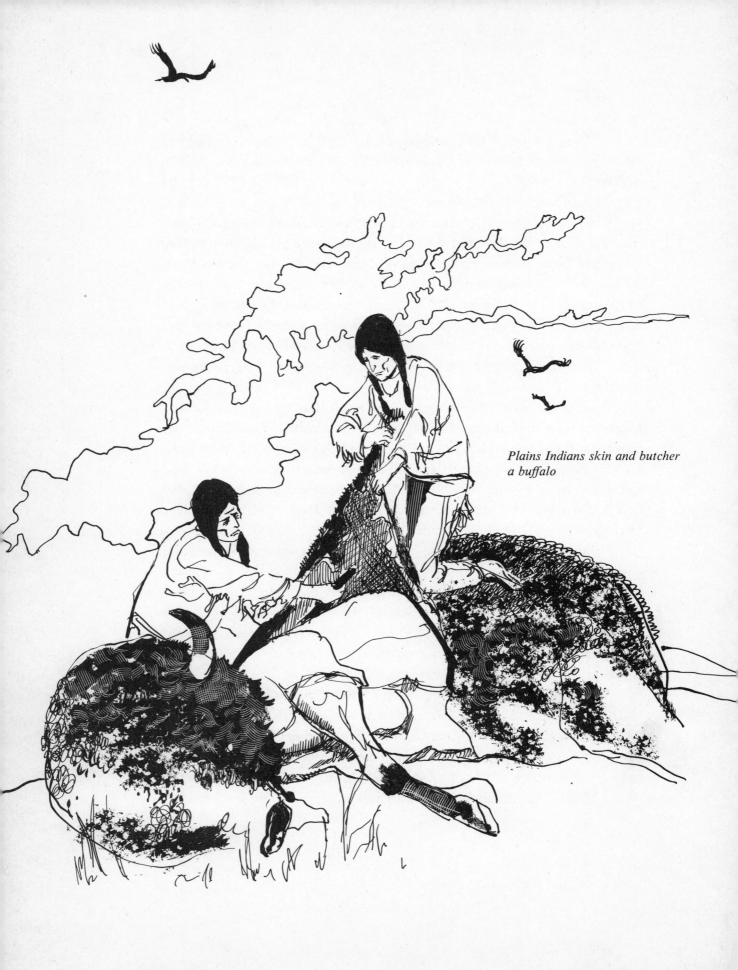

*Plains Indians skin and butcher
a buffalo*

was used for containers, thongs, saddles, clothing, and lodge coverings. The dried excrement, known as buffalo chips, was burned for cooking and heating. The bones, hoofs, and horns were made into cups, spoons, and ornaments.

Buffaloes were found throughout the great plains. They seemed to be unlimited in number. Some herds were said to have contained four million head. Witnesses said that one herd occupied a piece of land fifty miles long and twenty-five miles wide. Remember, this was only one herd.

Comanche hunts conducted by the entire band took place during the early summer and late fall. This was because buffaloes were the fattest at these times and also because the hides were best for clothing in early summer and for robes in late fall. Everyone worked before, during, and after the hunt for a hunt was a major task. Scouts located the herd. Then camp had to be moved near the buffaloes. A hunt leader took over and directed all the activities. The well trained horses were a great help in chasing the buffaloes. The hunter would ride up behind a buffalo and shoot him with an arrow or stab him with a long-handled spear. Each dead buffalo was the property of the man who killed it. Extra buffaloes were killed to be given to those who had no one to hunt for them.

The heavy work of skinning and butchering was done by the men out on the plains. After they got the meat back to camp, the women took over and cooked what they needed then and preserved the rest.

Although the buffalo was the chief source of meat, elk, black bear, and deer were also used. Food was usually plentiful but if it did become scarce one of the horses was eaten. Cattle were also captured in raids, but were either traded or eaten on the spot.

Certain foods were tabu. That is, they were avoided because of what was thought might happen if they were eaten. Pigs were not eaten because they were associated with mud. Turkey would make one cowardly and cause one to run from his enemy.

Meat was generally cooked by holding it over the fire on a stick. Sometimes it was roasted right in the fire. Stews were made by boiling the meat in a leather pot using the heated-stone boiling method.

Their diet was varied by the wild vegetables and fruits collected by the women. These included persimmons, mulberries, plums, grapes, currants, berries, nuts, and potatoes. Honey was a great favorite as a food.

Visitors were served food whenever they arrived. Otherwise, a formal meal was prepared the first thing in the morning and a larger one was served in the evening. During the rest of the day people ate whatever they had when they were hungry. After each meal water was offered to all in order that they might rinse out their mouths and wash their hands.

Boys did not wear any clothes until they reached the age of eight or nine. Then they wore a breechclout, leggings, and moccasins. The leggings were often blue or red, their favorite colors, and decorated with teeth, beads, or silver. Moccasins were sometimes decorated the same way and might also have a fringe of fur. In the winter the men wore deer or mountain sheepskin shirts and boots with the fur inside.

The Comanche woman clothed herself in buckskin. Both skirts and blouse were soft and fringed. These were decorated with rows of beads and silver. Beaded moccasins completed the wardrobe. Young girls wore a breechclout until they grew up and then they wore adult clothing.

In the winter men and women wore buffalo robes for warmth. Both men and women painted their faces before meeting strangers and on special occasions. Women wore their hair loose and did not give it much attention but men spent considerable time in caring for theirs.

The tipi was the house of the Comanche. It was made of buffalo hides placed over poles in the same way that other plains Indians

154

built it. The women did all the work required to build the tipi.

The Comanche found time for recreation and entertainment. Evenings were often gay with dancing, singing, and story telling. These activities were both entertaining and educational. Competitive games took place in the daytime and were particularly enjoyed by the children and young people.

*Indian girl of the plains
with her toys*

BLACKFOOT

The Blackfoot Indians were known as the buffalo hunters of the North American Plains. This was because they lived on the great prairies, the natural home of the buffalo, and used the buffalo as one of their major sources of food and clothing. The buffalo lived there because of the tall, luxuriant grass.

Actually, these animals are not buffalo but American bison, but since buffalo has become the common name we will use it here.

The Blackfoot actually occupied the part of the plains now known as Alberta and Saskatchewan in Canada and the northern part of the state of Montana. The exact area was between the north branch of the Saskatchewan river and the Missouri river east of the Rocky Mountains.

The early Blackfoot were made up of three independent tribes that were friendly to each other. However, each had its own land, tribal organization, and ceremonials. Together they probably once numbered over ten thousand.

These northern hunters were tall. In skin color and facial features they looked more Mongoloid than their plains neighbors who had a more hawk-like facial appearance. Blackfoot eyes had a definite slant and their hair was black and straight.

After the Blackfoot were able to obtain horses by stealing, trading, and raising their own they were in a much better position to kill the plentiful buffalo. They became more dependent upon the buffalo and less on plant products and small game. With greater success in hunting they had more leisure time.

From then on, until the buffalo became scarce and the west more populated by white settlers, these and other plains Indians relied more and more on the buffalo and moved their camps in order to be near the big herds.

The buffalo dominated the activities of the Blackfoot. Every part of the animal was used and provided many things in addition to food. Hides dressed with the hair remaining made robes. Hides

156

Blackfoot tipis were often decorated with designs and story-telling pictures.

that had been thinned and had the hair removed with wood-ash lye were turned into shirts, leggings, moccasins, tipi covers and bags. When cut into strips the hides made ropes and lines. The buffalo hair was used to stuff pillows and saddles as well as for decorative purposes. The sinew was made into thread and string. The horns were softened by boiling and shaped into spoons. Bones were fashioned into tools to be used in dressing hides and in preparing food.

Hides were prepared either stiff or soft. For things requiring tough material such as shields, packing cases, and moccasin soles the hides were prepared stiff. This was done by pegging the skin out and scraping the fat, flesh and muscle tissue off with a bone tool. The skin was then left to cure, bleach, and harden in the sun. After hardening it was scraped to an even thickness. For clothes and tipi covers a soft finish was needed. This was secured by cleaning the hide and drying it as indicated and then rubbing a mixture of animal brains and fat into the hide with a smooth stone. Then it was again dried in the sun. Next it was soaked with warm water and rolled up for a few days. After this, the hide was rubbed over with a rough stone and sawed to and fro across a rope until it was dry and soft.

Shirts and dresses made from tanned skins were often decorated with strips of weasel skin. Tipi coverings were also made of the soft hides sewn together in the shape of a half circle. It required about two dozen buffalo hides to make a tipi fourteen feet across and ten feet high. The frame was of four pine or spruce poles tied together near the top with sinew. Then half a dozen more poles were set in between these in a circular pattern and also tied near the top. The hide covering was then lashed to one pole pulled around the frame and lashed again to the same pole. The bottom was pegged or weighted down with rocks. Poles were used to adjust the flaps for the smoke-hole vent. Entrance was made through a slit covered with a hide curtain.

It took a great deal of work to make a tipi and when a new

158

one was needed the woman invited a large number of friends to help her. During this time she fed them for helping her.

The inside of the tipi was lined with a piece of hide that hung down all around the edge. This prevented drafts and provided storage space. A fire was made in the center, under the smoke hole, within a ring of flat stones. Ceremonial materials were kept in the rear, the husband and wife slept on the left of the entrance, children and others slept on the right.

Carrying bags and storage bags were made of rawhide. The large ones were called *parfleche* by the white trappers who first saw them. These were large flat envelopes that were lashed together to keep the contents from falling out. The top flaps were carefully decorated. Fresh paunches and hides were used as vessels for stone-boiling meat and soups. To stone boil, stones were heated until they were red hot and then dropped into the vessel of soup or meat. A vessel was formed by pressing hide in a hole in the ground or by supporting it around the edges with short sticks to hold it in shape.

Usually fresh meat was available the year round. But pemmican was prepared after the bigger hunts in order to have food on hand in the event of poor hunting. The meat was prepared by first cutting it in thin strips and then drying it in the sun. When dry, the meat was slightly roasted, pounded into a meal and mixed with fat. This was then packed in parfleches and sealed with tallow. These were then placed in stone-lined pits and covered to protect them from animals.

The Blackfoot tribes operated as small bands centered around one or more of the male relatives except during the good hunting season. Upon marriage a woman went to live with her husband's band. Children belonged to the father's band. The number of bands and their size varied from time to time. Each band had its own name such as: *Solid Topnots, Sharp Whiskers, Skunks*, etc.

For the winter each band went to its own territory. Within its own territory each band had a favorite place, a sheltered valley

*Typical burial custom
of the plains Indians*

or hollow, that offered protection from the winter storms. At this season of the year buffalo were killed by driving them over cliffs.

In order to be sure of a successful hunt the Blackfoot constructed what was known as a buffalo pound. The pound itself was under a cliff. A long runway with post and brush fences on each side was constructed to lead to the top of the cliff.

The area under the cliff was fenced in with the same kind of post and brush fence. Buffaloes were coaxed into the runway by men wearing buffalo masks. Once the animals were in the runway they were chased over the cliff by other Indians who had been hiding in the brush. Buffaloes not killed by the fall were shot by bow and arrow or struck with stones or clubs.

After the killing, all the animals were skinned and cut up. Men, women, children, and dogs all helped to carry the meat back to camp. After horses became available they were used both in chasing the buffalo into the pounds and in carrying the meat back to camp.

In the summer, the various bands assembled into their tribal groups. Buffaloes were hunted by men who formed large hunting parties. The combined hunting parties made it possible to drive larger herds greater distances and to kill more of the animals. In addition to the pounds used in the winter they sometimes burned the dry prairie grass to chase the buffaloes in the direction they wanted them to go.

For the tribal gathering that took place in the summertime, camp was made in a great circle with a large opening to the east. Tipis were set up three or four deep in a circle of perhaps a half-mile across. Each band camped in the same place in the circle each year.

Each man was a member of a society that performed dances and ceremonies. Each society had its own name, songs, dances, and rank. Members of each society were about the same age.

Approximately every four years they transferred the rights of their society to the next younger group. At the same time, members

161

of this group received the rights of the men in the group four years older. This was something like moving from one grade to the other in school, the big difference being that in this case one had to buy one's position from another person. This was done by the payments of such items as robes, horses, or weapons. In one group of the Blackfoot a boy would start as a *pigeon* then move to a *mosquito* and after seven more moves finally become a *bull,* the top group. By this time he was an old man and stayed a *bull* until he died.

The summer camp provided an opportunity for ceremonial activities. The societies put on feasts and ceremonies between the communal hunts. The Blackfoot believed that it was the dances and rituals that made the hunt successful. Hunting was usually good during this season and much food was preserved for later use.

The last ceremonial of the season was the Sun Dance at which individuals and the tribe as a whole sought power and protection. This lasted for a week or more and at the end of it the camp broke up and the bands moved towards their winter quarters.

Because of the movement of entire bands from winter to summer camps and back again, a transportation system was necessary. Before the horse, two different means were used. One was to pack the household utensils and other possessions on their own backs. The other was by the use of the travois, two poles lashed together and harnessed onto the shoulders of a dog. Then the load was placed on slats that had been lashed across the poles. After the Blackfoot secured horses the travoises were made larger and could support much larger tipi covers. As more horses became available, different kinds of harnesses and saddles were designed and used.

The use of horses not only made buffalo hunting easier but also made it easier and more profitable to engage in raiding. Actually, it was through raiding that many a young Blackfoot got his horses. Horses were also acquired through trade and by capturing those running wild.

162

Blackfoot mountain chief

PAIUTE

The Paiute occupied the arid plateau of the Great Basin which is between the Columbia and Colorado rivers. This area is now included in parts of the present states of California, Nevada, Oregon, and Utah.

The Great Basin receives very little rainfall; however, the mountains to the west and east receive considerable snow and are covered for many months. The streams depend upon this snow for their water.

The summers of this area are very hot and the winters bitter cold. Frost may continue for several weeks each winter.

Hardwood trees are found in the mountains and soft woods on the lower ranges. Grass covers the lower mountain slopes. On the basin floor can be found bunches of grass, sagebrush and other scrub. This vegetation is interspersed with stretches of salt and stony gravel.

In the eighteen hundreds the largest band of Paiute generally consisted of about a hundred persons who occupied a territory of about fifty to a hundred square miles. Other bands were smaller in size. In the winter the bands gathered together. In the spring they broke up into family groups and roamed the territory.

In the winter these Indians lived in houses called *wikiups*. These wikiups were conical in shape and were made of a pole frame covered with bark strips, dried brush, or reeds. The top was left open to provide an outlet for the smoke of the fire which was kept in a pit in the center of the floor.

Each winter settlement usually had a sweat-house that had been built near a stream. This sweat-house was sometimes a domed-shaped shelter covered with skins or grass. Water was poured on hot stones to form steam and the men sweated in this house before bathing in the river. The sweating was believed to have medicinal values and was associated with their religious beliefs.

During the summer the Paiute left these camps and built roofs

164

Big game was scarce in Paiute country. Neighboring camps sometimes joined together to conduct a rabbit drive.

of grass and brush that were supported on four or more poles. No sides were used but wind screens were constructed. A fireplace was built on the inside of the wind screen.

Since large game was scarce, vegetable foods, insects and small animals were the main foods. The seeds of grass, wild rye, rice grass, and sunflower were collected. Berries, wild onions, and clovers were eaten fresh. Pointed sticks were used to dig tiger lily, spike rush, and other bulbs.

On occasions they diverted various streams so as to water wild plants for better production. Grasshoppers, lizards, and tortoises were caught during the summer. Grasshoppers were considered a delicacy and were boiled and roasted. Pine nuts were gathered in the fall. They could be kept for long periods of time and used when other food supplies ran out.

Women did most of the collecting. Seeds, from various grasses, were beaten into small baskets which in turn were emptied into larger baskets. When shaken into the air the wind blew the grass away. The seeds were then dried by being shaken up in baskets containing live coals. These dried seeds were crushed and ground on flat square stones with a cylindrical stone which was rolled over the seeds like a rolling pin.

Supplies of dried seeds, berries, nuts, and roots were packed in skin bags which in turn were buried in grass-lined pits at the winter settlement.

Small game hunted included squirrels, gophers, rats, and rabbits. Neighboring camps joined together to conduct rabbit drives. These sometimes lasted ten days and were under the direction of a "Rabbit Boss" who directed the party. Each day a party of about thirty to fifty people would drive all the rabbits they could scare up into a semicircular net that was about four feet high and over one hundred feet long. When the rabbits became caught in the mesh they were killed with clubs.

Ducks, mud-hens and geese were hunted on the lakes. Although

Piaute Indians making a fire

not very plentiful, antelope, mountain sheep, and deer were hunted with bow and arrow. Each man made his own bow and arrows.

Fish were caught in the lakes and streams. Double-barbed hooks of deer bone were used with lines. Sometimes fish were lured to the bank at night with torches and then speared with a two-pronged spear.

The Paiute made extensive use of animal hides. The skin of the rabbit was removed in one piece and then cut in long strips. Then the strips were twisted together and dried. When dry they were woven into a rabbit-skin blanket. This blanket provided a warm wrap for protection against the winter winds. It took about fifty skins to make a five foot square blanket.

Many Paiute went completely naked in the summer although some women wore aprons of milkweed fiber and men a breechclout and leggings of buckskin when traveling. In the winter everyone wore cloaks of animal skins. Soft-soled deer hide moccasins were worn. Circular snow shoes made of a wooden frame with crosspieces of bent willow were used for winter travel over the snow.

The Paiute were experts at basketry. Split willow twigs were the major materials used. Baskets were either made by weaving or coiling and binding with grasses. Baskets that were woven were made by weaving one set of twigs over and under a framework of twigs made in the shape of the basket. In coiling and binding, the twigs were coiled around and around on top of each other. Each layer was bound to the one before with strong grass. Patterns were worked in by using other materials or by staining the willows. Caps, seed beaters, and large carrying baskets were woven. Trays that needed strength and bottles that were to hold water were made by coiling. These were sometimes strengthened and waterproofed with pitch.

A few of the bands made pottery. Knives and arrow points were chipped from obsidian. In a small fiber bag that hung at his waist, every Paiute carried an obsidian knife that was about five or six inches long, and a fire-making kit.

A couple could marry as long as they were not known to be related. This meant that a person married into another band. The couple stayed with the wife's family in her band until they had children when they usually moved to the husband's family band.

Piaute woman making a warm rabbit-skin robe

DAKOTA

The Dakota, also known as the Sioux, because they belong to the Siouan family, are what many people think of as typical Indians. This is because they wore eagle-feather war bonnets, hunted buffalo, and savagely fought the settlers. For over 200 years the Dakota were free and independent, living as nomadic warriors and hunters in the northern plains. Then in 1855, under General Harvey, the United States Army waged a twenty year battle to round them up and put them on reservations. Finally, a treaty was agreed upon by most of the Dakota tribes and they moved to the Great Sioux Reservation of South Dakota. The Dakota had little choice but to accept the agreement for the buffalo and other sources of food were vanishing from the plains.

This is the largest group speaking the Siouan language and is divided according to its movement into *Santee, Yankton,* and *Teton*. The Santee division lived in the northern plains and was noted among the Lake Tribes. They called themselves *Dakota*. The Yankton division called themselves *Nakota* and lived in eastern Dakota. The western Sioux called *Lakota* lived west of the Missouri River.

These Indians used picture writing to tell a story, to record the events that happened in past years, important ceremonials and treaties. These calendars were painted on deer, antelope, or buffalo hides.

Vests appeared early in colonial times and were highly favored by the Dakota. It was a windbreaker as well as an ornament.

The bowl of the Dakota pipe is at a right angle to the stem and has a solid projection extending in front of the bowl.

A boat used by the Indian women of the Dakota tribe was known as the bull-boat. It was a tub-shaped vessel of willow frame covered with rawhide. The women used it to carry their goods down or across the river. It was so light that when one was emptied, a woman could take it on her back and make her way across the land.

170

Dakota women with tub-shaped
bull-boats

While subsistence of the people was largely derived from hunting and fishing, or from the wild fruits of the earth, yet many of these Indians farmed. The Dakota raised crops of corn, beans, and squash. Rows of small hills were made and three or four corn kernels were planted in each hill. In some cases a small piece of fish was added to the hill for fertilizer. The Dakotas boiled their food in buffalo stomachs or in rawhide bags.

The Dakota had picturesque costumes on which they used many different kinds of feathers. These feathers were cut or arranged to signify many different things. A Dakota's feathers could say, *killed an enemy* or *wounded many*. Their deeds could be identified by the kinds of feathers they wore.

In 1658 they had towns on the Mississippi, Missouri, and Saint Croix rivers. The biggest attack against the whites was under Little Crow in 1862. Fourteen years later, when gold was discovered, they rose again. This ended in the battle of Little Big Horn where Custer made his last stand. The Dakotas' last attempt to free themselves from the whites came after the Ghost Dance of 1890-1891. On this occasion they were beaten.

172

Once a plains warrior had won the right to wear another eagle feather he sometimes set out to secure it for himself.

SHEEP EATERS

The Sheep Eaters were a tribe of Indians that became extinct about one hundred years ago. At one time twenty-eight bands of these proud and happy people lived high in the mountains of Wyoming and Montana far removed from all other Indians. The only evidence of these Indians that remains today are the inscriptions upon walls of granite rock, a few arrow heads, and the great shrine wheel on Bald Mountain where all the bands gathered to worship the sun, twice a year.

Their name, Sheep Eaters, came from the fact that the mountain sheep were their principal source of food. However, during the winter elk and deer were often killed.

They lived in the grassy parks of the mountains that were kept green by the fresh spring water. Evergreen and quaking aspen trees were plentiful. Granite walls rose on the sides of the valleys from fifty to a thousand feet high.

Tipis of these Indians were made quite differently from those of other Indian tribes. Instead of being covered with rawhide they were thatched with quaking aspen bark and either covered with a gum and glue made from sheep hoofs or with gum made from pitch pine.

They believed in many gods. A major god was the sun. Their lives were devoted to these gods with the idea that their eternal happiness would be complete in a great Happy Region beyond where all is bright and warm.

The great wheel, which was the shrine of these people was plotted on the ground. It was eighty feet across the face and had twenty-eight spokes representing the twenty-eight different bands. At the center there was a house of stone that was for the chief. Facing the northeast was the house of the god of plenty, facing southeast was the house of the goddess of beauty, and to the west was the granite cave dedicated to the sun god. The worshippers stood along the spokes and chanted their songs of praise.

174

A woman 115 years old, believed to be the last of the Sheep Eaters, was asked what had happened to the rest of her people. She said that one day a sick white man came into her village and was taken care of by the medicine man. The white man died and soon many Indians got sick and died. Some ran to other villages, others to the mountains. Pretty soon the people were dying in all the villages. The few that were left wandered down out of the mountains and went to live with other Indian tribes. The Sheep Eaters were no more.

*There is evidence of
prehistoric Indians
in the Ohio region*

Chapter VI / INDIANS OF THE EASTERN WOODLANDS

THE VARIOUS TRIBES of Indians of the eastern woodlands, sometimes called the eastern forests, lived in an area that extended from the Atlantic Ocean to the Mississippi River, and from New Brunswick, Canada, to Florida. This entire area was occupied by one or another of the eastern woodland tribes at the time the white man first started to settle there; except for the portion that is now known as the states of Kentucky, West Virginia, and the southern portions of Indiana and Ohio. This part of the land was probably uninhabited in the early historical period.

Very little is known about the ancient history of the eastern woodland area because the damp forests swallowed up the Indian villages and the art objects made of wood. Huts, canoes, baskets, and other wooden objects decayed many years ago. Only a few stone, pottery and shell objects such as weapons, tools and pots remained.

Early man roamed the eastern coast when mastodons and mammoths lived there. They survived by hunting, fishing, and gathering seeds, nuts, and fruits. They lived in caves and under rocky ledges. During these prehistoric years many tribes who spoke different languages roamed the area. The Iroquois, one of the largest groups, lived in and around what is now New York State. Another large group was the Algonquin-speaking tribes who lived in the areas now known as New England, the Great Lakes region, and down the Atlantic coast. Many other smaller groups occupied the southern part of the coastal area.

Shell heaps along the Atlantic coast from Canada to Florida show where some of these tribes lived. Some time after the birth of

Christ they learned how to plant and use corn. Later on, they grew garden crops such as squash and beans. At this time they also learned how to make pots and bowls out of clay.

The villages were on hill tops and often surrounded by wooden walls for protection. The women tended the crops, wove baskets, dressed skins for clothes, and made clay pots. The men made bows, arrows, and spears with which they hunted. They also fished and spent much time in religious activities. A considerable amount of time was spent in hunting, fishing, and food gathering.

This section of the country, the eastern woodlands, was much better watered than the southwest. Forests of hardwoods in the north and pine in the south provided wood and cover for game but were difficult to clear for agriculture without metal tools.

When white man first contacted the various Indian groups of the eastern woodlands they were speaking four basic languages. Algonkian, the most widely spoken, was used by tribes from Canada to Virginia. Iroquoian was spoken by the tribes of that name and by others in New York and in the south. Muskogean was the language of groups from Virginia to Florida. Siouan, a plains language, was the language of other tribes.

Farming was done near the streams and in the valleys because of the easy access to water. The hoe was used in the cultivation of crops. Gardening was a woman's work. Hunting was very important in this area. These Indians hunted turkey, deer, and some bear. Hunting was considered a man's work, and was done with a long bow and arrow.

Shellfish were also an important food for those along the coast. Fishing was done by spearing and poisoning. Wild plant products, such as artichoke roots and nuts, were eaten.

Dressed skins, mainly that of the deer, were used for clothing. Men wore a breechclout, fringed leggings, jacket, and soft-soled moccasins. Women wore a short-sleeved dress of skin, and in cold weather they wore a skin robe.

Shell heaps along the Atlantic coast show where some of these early tribes lived

IROQUOIS

The Iroquois roamed the eastern woodlands from the time of Columbus to the arrival of the pilgrims at Plymouth. On arrival of the white man in northern New York, he found the Iroquois Indians occupying the lake region and Mohawk valley. The various Iroquois tribes occupied the area from the Great Lakes south to North Carolina.

The French who arrived later described the Iroquois as savages. In their homes, however, they were noted for their good humor, generosity, and intelligence. During this period of time they lived in permanent villages, each group farming his own plot of land.

It was about the year 1570, when weakened by war with their neighbors, the Algonquian, and their own kinsmen, that five tribes united for protection. These five tribes, later known as the Five Nations formed the famous "League of the Iroquois" which occupied an area across northern New York. They were the Mohawks, the Oneidas, the Onondagas, the Cayugas, and the Senecas. The Tuscaroras joined later.

The climate of this area was temperate with four separate seasons. With good rainfall and a long warm summer it was possible for these Indians to engage in agriculture.

Animals such as the bear, deer, moose, wolf, fox, raccoon, porcupine, beaver, hare, and squirrel were known. Forests of pine, spruce, hemlock, cedar, elm, oak, maple, chestnut, and hickory covered the hills.

The Iroquois, tall with light, coppery-brown skin, straight black hair, and black eyes, spoke Iroquoian. Other Iroquois-speaking tribes were the Hurons, Neutrals, Eries, and Conestoga.

They used pictographs and animal figures to describe battles and other activities. Agreements were made and recorded by strings of wampum as were certain events and ceremonials. The term *wampum* means *string of white beads* in the Algonquian language. These beads were made from mollusk shells. It was an object of barter and a symbol of sincerity. Certain officials were keepers of the

180

Mohawks, Oneidas, Onondagas, Cayugas and Senecas joined to form the famous "League of the Iroquois." The Tuscaroras joined later.

wampum. They also remembered the terms of treaties or other events that went with each string of wampum. Once a year they recited these events to all members of the tribe at a tribal assembly.

Mushrooms and a variety of edible roots, leaves, and shoots were gathered and eaten. A kind of bread was made from dried, ground and pulverized maple bark, pond lily roots, wild parsnips, and groundnuts. In the fall all kinds of nuts were collected and used in the many different dishes that they cooked. Wild grapes, cherries, plums, and all kinds of berries were eaten fresh and also dried, pressed into cakes, and mixed with other food.

Maple trees were tapped for the syrup which was boiled and made into maple syrup and sugar. The eggs of quail, partridge, and wild duck were collected and eaten, if possible just before they were ready to hatch. Frogs, turtles, crayfish, and clams were also eaten. Raw ants were choice items of food because of their acid flavor.

Before going on a hunt men fasted, bathed, and offered sacrifices. They also relied on charms and dreams to bring them success on the hunt. The chief weapon was the bow and arrow. Arrows were about three feet long with a head of bone, horn or chipped stone. Feathers on the other end caused the arrow to stay steady in flight. Arrows were carried in a quiver slung over the back. The bow had a special shape with a reverse curve in the middle or recurved ends. They were about four feet long and powerful enough to put an arrow into an animal's skull.

Animals were either hunted individually with the bow and arrow or caught in traps, snares, and pitfalls. In spring the Iroquois fished for salmon, sturgeon, trout, and eels. Bone hooks, traps, nets, and spears were used. Harpoon and bow and arrow were also favorite means of fishing.

Most of the food they ate came from their farms, which were as large as several hundred acres near some of the villages. The main crop was maize known as Indian corn. Several kinds were grown including those similar to our sweet corn and popcorn. Along with

182

*Iroquois woman grinding corn
outside the long house*

the corn they planted beans, squash and pumpkins.

Land was cleared by cutting down the trees and then burning over the entire area. A hoe was used to loosen up the soil and chop down the weeds. This hoe probably was made by fastening a piece of deer antler or deer shoulder blade on a strong stick. In planting, a hole was made with a digging stick, a few seeds dropped in, and then covered with dirt. Each hole was fertilized with fish, when abundant.

Venison and other meats were preserved by drying and smoking. Squash and pumpkins were also dried. All of these were stored in underground pits that had been lined with bark. Meat and fish were usually broiled or boiled in earthen pots.

It is said that the Iroquois had over fifty ways of preparing corn in combination with other food items. These included such dishes as corn soup, boiled corn, corn pudding, and corn meal made into cakes with maple sugar.

These Indians had only one regular cooked meal each day and this was at about ten or eleven o'clock in the morning. The men ate first and the women and children last. At other times of the day people helped themselves to soup or cold hominy whenever they were hungry.

Cooking utensils and pipes were made from pottery. Pots were made by the coil method, which is to roll clay out like a rope and then coil it into the shape of the pot. The pot was then smoothed by hand, dried in the sun and baked hard in a slow fire.

When they wanted to go some place on land they walked. In the winter they traveled on snowshoes. Birchbark canoes were used on the many lakes and rivers.

Villages had from three hundred to three thousand persons. These villages were usually located near a lake, stream, or spring.

The houses were called "long houses" because they were from fifty to one hundred feet long, twenty to thirty feet wide, and twenty to thirty feet in height. Each house had a frame of poles. An arched

The Iroquois rattle dance of the False Face Society was supposed to drive away illness.

roof was supported by rafters that were bent. Both the roof and side walls were covered with slabs of dried elm bark. Poles were tied over the bark to hold it in place.

Inside the house, fires were built about every twenty feet. Each fire served two families, that is the family living on each side of the house opposite a fire. Boxes of supplies separated one family from another.

The Iroquois used no metal and disliked working in stone. However, they did use stone for ax heads and arrow points. Needles, punches, knives, and combs were made from bone and horn. Clamshells served as knives and spoons. Scrapers, spoons, and dishes were carved from wood.

They did some work in textiles such as woven baskets of rushes and corn husks. Cords, bags, and fish nets were also woven of the same materials. They did not make cloth but used skins for all their clothing.

In the summer the men wore a breechclout and the women wore a long kilt. During the winter both the men and women added a short sleeveless shirt, a kilt that extended to the knees, leggings, moccasins and an outer robe of furs.

For ornaments they used necklaces of shells, stone or bone beads, and animal teeth. On ceremonial occasions a man wore knee rattles of deer hoofs and a headdress of feathers.

The Iroquois carried on trade with neighboring tribes. The men used to hunt, fish, wage war, make weapons, build houses, make canoes, construct snowshoes, manufacture utensils and assist the women with the crops.

The women did most of the agricultural work, and also cooked, kept house, took care of the children, gathered plant products, collected firewood, preserved the meat and fish, and made the clothing. Both men and women worked cooperatively with others of the same sex to get the job done.

Although the women did most of the work they were not under

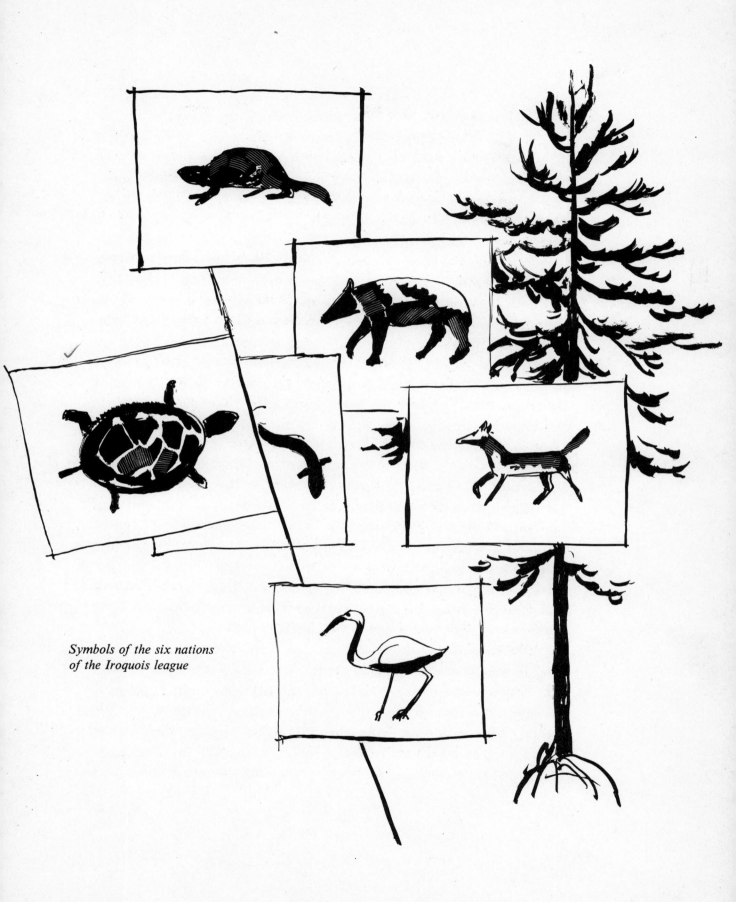

Symbols of the six nations
of the Iroquois league

the authority of the men. The women owned the homes and all of their goods. When a man got married he went to live in the house of his wife's mother. In this house his wife was given a place for them to live. Everything was shared by members of the household.

A number of related households made up a clan. Each clan had its own chiefs. The clan chiefs made up the governing body of the tribe to which the clans belonged. Hunting grounds, fishing grounds, and such things as springs were owned by the tribe and available to all tribal members regardless of their clan. Some of the clans, such as the Bear, Wolf, and Turtle were in all five tribes of the Iroquois. Having fellow clan members in the various tribes helped to further bind these tribes together in the League of Iroquois.

The top governing body of all of Iroquois was the council of sachems. This was a group of fifty of the greatest chiefs from all of the tribes. Although the sachems were all men it was the women who nominated them for office. All important intertribal decisions were made at the sachem council.

War was an important matter for the Iroquois and any man that could get a band of followers could go on the warpath.

Preparation for war included a feast, a war dance, and consultation with their gods. The weapons included a tomahawk, knife, war club and bow and arrow. Warriors would sneak up on their enemies, preferably in the woods. If successful they would either scalp their victims or take them prisoner. If they scalped them they would then take the scalp home to preserve it by first scraping it clean and then drying over a fire.

The Iroquois never exchanged prisoners. When prisoners were captured and brought back to camp they were given to households that had lost a warrior. The other prisoners were either given to anyone that wanted them or they were tortured to death. The captives chosen for adoption were forced to run between parallel lines of men and women who would strike them with thorn branches. If they fell they were put to death. If they survived they were given

188

new names and adopted into one of the households.

When the Dutch opened a trading post in 1615 the Iroquois were able to get firearms in exchange for furs. With these weapons they soon conquered all their neighbor Indian tribes. By 1700 they had the most powerful Indian empire north of Mexico. The Iroquois did not get along with the French but worked closely with the English. Thus, they helped to keep the French away from the English colonies and helped the colonies in trade. The American Revolution brought their political independence to an end as they all had fought with the British except the Oneidas.

At the end of the war many of the Iroquois went to Canada where two thirds of the nation lives today. A few still live in New York on reservations.

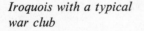

Iroquois with a typical war club

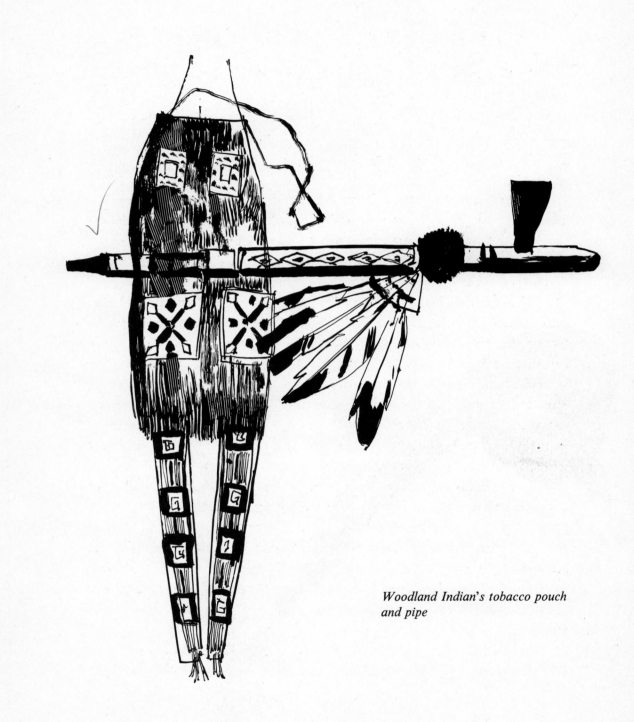

Woodland Indian's tobacco pouch and pipe

CHIPPEWA

The area now known as the state of Michigan was the chief residential area for the early Chippewa Indians. Chippewa being the popular term for the Ojibway Indians. When first contacted here by white man in about 1640, they were not very numerous, probably only a few hundred. By uniting themselves with other tribes around the great lakes and through natural increase they grew to over twenty-five thousand. They then spread over a much larger geographical area.

The Chippewa were a hospitable and proud people. In general, they were aloof and not readily approached by missionaries. They were brave warriors and respected by the other tribes. Most of the Chippewa were nomadic but some did stay in one place long enough to cultivate corn.

Those north of Lake Superior lived mostly by hunting, fishing, and gathering wild plants. They hunted away from the villages in the winter and cultivated gardens in the village in the summer. Those on the west end of Lake Superior raised corn and squash in the summer and hunted in the winter. Others spent the whole year at the lakes and lived chiefly on whitefish which they caught in the rapids of Sault Ste. Marie.

Beaver and moose were hunted along the southern shore of Lake Superior. Many bands wandered west and hunted buffalo, elk, and deer. Bows and arrows were used originally for hunting and later supplemented by guns traded to them by the white man.

Fishing was very important in the life of the Chippewa. Whitefish and sturgeon were most plentiful. Those bands who did not use some fish the year round gathered at the rivers for the run of whitefish in the fall. These fish were caught in nets that were fastened on the ends of poles. While standing in a canoe the Chippewa dipped in the fish.

In addition to fish, berries of all kinds and wild rice were substantial parts of the Chippewa diet. Blueberries, raspberries, and strawberries were eaten fresh and also dried for future use.

Wild rice was common in most of the territory occupied by the Chippewa. The rice grains were collected by women in two canoes working together. One woman would bend the plants down into her partner's canoe with a long pole. The partner then beat the grain off the plant and into the canoe. Then the process was reversed with the plants being bent in the other direction and the grain beaten into the other canoe. In this way the rice grain could be collected by the bushel.

It was an advantage for the Sioux and Chippewa to have a treaty of peace, for the Chippewa needed to share the hunting grounds of the Sioux and, in return, the Sioux were able to trade with the French through the Chippewa who acted as agents for them.

For shelter the Chippewa built tipis or cabins. These tipis and cabins consisted of frames covered with strips of birch bark that were sewn together. Small families used the tipi. Larger families, or two or more families living together, used cabins.

Openings at the top of both of these structures provided light and escape for smoke from the cooking fire.

The clothes of the Chippewa were of skins of animals such as the deer and elk. These were dehaired and tanned. In the winter, robes of furs were added for warmth. The men wore a breechclout, leggings, and moccasins. The women wore knee length leggings, a short skirt, a blouse, and moccasins. In the summer children wore little or no clothing.

Each person had his own guardian spirit. To find his individual spirit a child, on reaching the age of ten or twelve, fasted for several days so that a dream would come to him. Each morning the child was asked what had occurred during the night. The child kept fasting until he remembered something that happened in regard to the sun, thunder or some other occurrence. Thus, he was able to decide upon his spirit.

In addition, all persons paid special attention to the spirits that

192

A Chippewa offered tobacco to spirits which he believed were living in the sun, rocks, rivers and animals.

they believed were living in such things as the sun, rocks, and rivers. Offerings were made to the spirits of these objects. Tobacco would be tossed into the lakes and dogs were sacrificed.

The *midewiwin,* or medicine dance, was one of the most important curing devices. It was used as a means of recovering health or as thanksgiving for continuing good health. This dance pointed up the relation of these Indians to the supernatural forces. The midewiwin was given only once a year with only members being permitted to attend the entire ceremony. Membership was limited to carefully selected men and women candidates who could also pay the high initiation fees. First came a period of purification in the medicine lodge. Then a public performance. Those to be initiated hung clothes or cloth on a cross that was placed outside the medicine lodge. After that members of the society initiated the newcomers into the society at a ceremony held in the lodge. In this ceremony the initiate was shown a small white shell which was the chief emblem of the society. This was accompanied by the swinging of rattles while the four initiating priests ran around the lodge and circled the initiates. Older Indians who practiced the midewiwin ceremony said that it was given to them by the gods years ago when many Indians were suffering from sickness and death.

Chippewa child on a cradle board

MENOMINEE

The Menominee Indians of Wisconsin believed that they originated from a Great Bear and other spirit beings of animal form. They belong to the Woodland culture area type as they were descendants of the Algonquian.

They occupied a number of villages on and near the Menominee River. The area itself was cut up by a number of small streams with numerous small lakes and swampy areas. These either drained eastward into Lake Michigan or westward into the Mississippi River.

In the early days the greatest part of the area was covered with forests that included birch, basswood, oak, cedar, and hickory trees. These forests produced a great variety of nuts, berries, and edible roots. Wild rice was probably the most important plant product. The forests abounded with bear, deer, and birds such as the eagle and the crane. Fish were plentiful in all the streams, especially sturgeon. Their economic life centered around fishing and gathering wild rice.

Fishing was the main occupation during the early years. Fish were caught by netting, trapping, and spearing from canoes or from the banks of streams. After the white fur traders came, hunting replaced fishing as furs were in great demand. Hunting was done by individuals, families, or small groups depending upon what was to be hunted and how much was needed. In hunting many magical aids were used such as "hunting bundles." These were packets of charms and fetishes that were devoted to the bear and other animals from which the people were supposed to have descended.

The Menominee believe that two foods were given to them by the spirit powers for their special use. These were maple sugar and wild rice. Both are seasonal. The maple sugar was made from maple sap in the spring and wild rice was harvested when ripe in the fall.

Little has been recorded about Menominee clothing at the time the white man first contacted them. It is known, however, that they did rub oil and grease on their hair and bodies. On special occasions colors were also applied. These dyes were made from berries and

The Menominee hunted the bear in family groups in northern Wisconsin.

roots. Garments for the men included moccasins, breechclout, and leggings. For the women there were moccasins, cloth skirt, waist, and leggings. The garments of both men and women had numerous beads and ribbons on them. In addition, each Indian usually wore earrings, necklaces, and a headdress of fur or feathers.

Houses were of two types. In the summer rectangular bark cabins were used, and in the winter they lived in domed lodges of mats or bark. Some houses had raised beds round the walls. In other cases, beds consisted of skins placed on the floor. The fireplace was in the center of the cabin or lodge.

The roads of these Indians were the streams, rivers, and lakes, which were traveled by canoe. Birchbark canoes were most common but some dugouts were also used. When traveling on land they wore moccasins and in winter made use of snowshoes.

Menominee weapons included: bows and arrows, clubs, knives of stone, shell, or bone, and axes of stone. These were all made by the men as were the sacred and ceremonial objects such as pipes and drums. The women made household utensils such as bowls, spoons and dishes from reeds and shells. In general, men hunted and made the canoes, while women did the cooking and made the clothes.

*Osceola, famous
Seminole chief*

SEMINOLE

The Seminole are the only Indians east of the Mississippi River whose culture and traditions have been preserved up to recent years. They lived and still live in a great section of the lower peninsula of Florida known as the Everglades. This is a vast area of swampland and water that takes in all of Florida south of Lake Okeechobee except a portion of land on the Atlantic ocean. Although the Everglade country is considered subtropical because of its geographical location, it really looks tropical to the observer. All kinds of tropical plants and animals thrive here. All of the Everglades is not swamp, however, for it contains numerous pine woods, grass marshes, and other open areas.

The Seminole and other Indians planted their crops in the rich loamy soil of the high elevations that jutted out of the swamp. It was into these areas that they fled to seek refuge from the white man.

The Seminole Indians were preceded by four major tribes called the Calusa, Tekesta, Timucua and Apalachee. These were practically wiped out by early explorers and settlers. Those who remained joined up with tribes from the north that fled south to Florida. In 1775 a group of Georgia Creek Indians called Muskogees entered Florida and became the nucleus for the Indians now known as the Seminole.

During the Revolutionary War the British used both the Seminole of Florida and the Creek of Georgia as soldiers against the Americans. When the British left Florida and Spain again took over, the Seminole lived peacefully. After the United States bought Florida from Spain in 1821 the Indians were forcefully put on reservations. The land they were given was the poorest available, as the white Americans wanted the best for themselves. As a result there were many Indian uprisings and many persons were killed and towns burned. To put the Florida Seminoles under our government it cost approximately one life and $10,000 for every Seminole man, woman, and child killed, or moved to the new territory.

200

Seminole Indians hunted in the Everglades with a blow gun which replaced the bow and arrow.

OTTAWA AND POTAWATOMI

The Ottawa and Potawatomi Indians had a very similar culture. In about 1600 the Ottawa occupied northeastern Michigan and Ontario, Canada, on the shores of Lake Huron. To escape the Iroquois the Ottawa moved westward, farther into Michigan. The Potawatomi were living in Michigan and Wisconsin and by 1700 had moved south and had become the dominant tribe in the Chicago area. Both tribes were divided into bands.

In summer both the Ottawa and Potawatomi lived in villages and farmed. In the fall they separated into family groups and went to the winter hunting grounds where they stayed until spring.

The hunting and fishing was done by the men. They hunted deer, elk, bear, beaver, and muskrat with bow and arrow, spears, snares, and traps. Fish were caught by hooks and lines, nets, and spears. The women did the gardening and collected plant products. Digging sticks and wooden hoes were used in the planting of the crops. The vegetable products collected included nuts, roots, berries, and wild rice. Both men and women collected the sap of maple trees and made it into sugar.

The homes in the permanent summer villages were either dome-shaped wigwams made of saplings and covered with mats, or large bark-covered houses. These villages were located on the waterways so they could travel by canoe. The dome-shaped wigwams were also used at the winter hunting grounds. Woven mats served as chairs or beds when spread on wooden platforms.

Big wooden mortars and pestles were used for pounding corn into meal. Other utensils found in the wigwams were woven bags, baskets, boxes or trunks of rawhide, wooden bowls, and pottery jars.

The pottery was made of clay tempered with particles of granitic stone. Tools included knives and scrapers of chipped flint, awls and needles of bone, and bow drills for making fire by friction. Musical instruments were drums, rattles, flutes, and whistles.

In the winter these Indians traveled on snowshoes or toboggans.

Pontiac, Ottawa chief

During the rest of the year they used birchbark canoes.

Tanned animal skins were used for clothing. Both men and women wore moccasins of skin, and fur robes, some of which were woven of strips of rabbit fur. Men wore leggings, garters, breech-clouts, belts, shirts, and hats or feathers. Women wore leggings, skirts, and shirts.

Both tribes were divided into a number of bands. Each band had its own territory and was independent of the other bands. However, they were related by language, clan, and marriage. Every tribal member belonged to a clan. Each band had members that belonged to different clans. Thus a person was related to individuals in other bands as well as in his own band. One could not marry a member of the same clan.

The religion of the Ottawa and Potawatomi centered around beliefs and practices involving the idea of a "Great Spirit," with lesser spirits such as fire, sun, and sea. It was believed that the human body had one spirit, and at death it followed the trail over the Milky Way to the heaven in the west. They had a "Grand Medicine Society" whose members were supposed to heal the sick and prolong life. Clans and societies had sacred bags, medicine bundles, and charms, as well as rituals that gave power to those that were charged with curing the sick.

Both the Ottawa and Potawatomi lived in villages and farmed during the summer months.

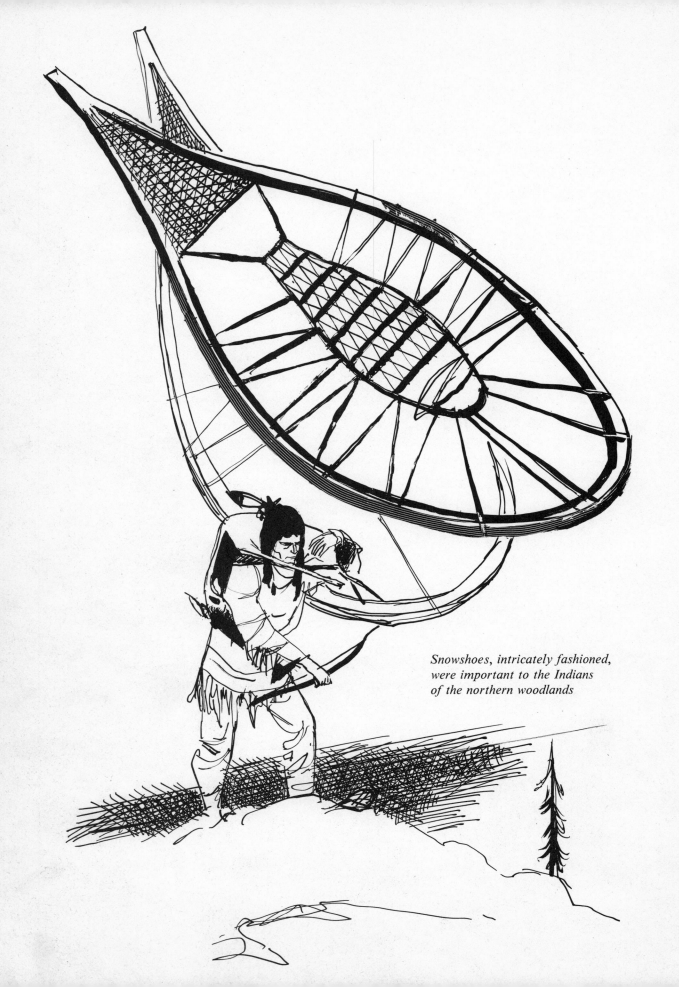

Snowshoes, intricately fashioned, were important to the Indians of the northern woodlands

SAUK, FOX, AND MIAMI

The Indians of the Sauk, Fox, and Miami tribes, during the years 1650-1760, lived in the western and southern parts of the Lake Michigan drainage area.

The Sauk and Fox lived, for the most part, in the northern Wisconsin forests.

The Miami lived in the area where the states of Wisconsin, Illinois, Indiana, and Michigan surround the lower end of Lake Michigan. This was a land of forests and tall-grass prairies. By 1700 some of the bands of these three tribes left the area to engage in the fur trade with the Europeans.

In the summer, from about April to October, they lived in permanent villages. When winter came they went to hunt buffalo on the plains. At this time they lived in temporary camps. Their food supply was based on farming and hunting.

The women did the farming by planting corn, beans, and squash. The fields were first cleared by burning and then the spots of ground to be planted had the dirt loosened with a digging stick or hoe of wood, shell, or bone. The women kept the birds away and also harvested the corn. Wild rice that grew in the area was also harvested by the women. Five bushels of rice and corn was considered a year's supply for a family. Extra grain was stored in pits in the ground that had been lined with bark.

After the grains were harvested entire villages moved to the prairies to hunt the buffalo. Everybody went except the old people who could not walk that distance. All had to hunt together. The dry prairie grass was set afire in a circle around the buffalo except for one place. As the buffalo ran out this place to escape the fire the Indians shot them with their bows and arrows. In some cases they killed as many as two hundred buffaloes a day in this way. The animals would be divided among the families taking part in the hunt. The meat would then be cut up and dried to preserve it.

While living at their villages they would sometimes take short hunting trips to get elk, deer, bear, and beaver.

The villages of the Sauk, Fox, and Miami were made up of groups of elongated wigwams. The frames of these were made of saplings inserted in the ground, bent over, and tied together in the center. This provided a dome-shaped roof over which were tied many mats of woven rushes. Each village had a council house that was much larger than the other homes but was erected in the same way.

Traveling was usually done on foot. The women carried their food, clothing, and other possessions on their backs by using head bands and pack straps. Sometimes the Sauk and Fox used dugout canoes.

All three tribes wore the same type of clothing. In the summer the men wore breechclouts and moccasins. In the winter they added shirts, leggings made of deer or elk skin, and buffalo skin robes with the fur left on them. The summer clothing for the women was a kind of skirt apron and moccasins. In the winter they added leggings and an outer skirt of skin plus the buffalo skin robe. Robes were sometimes painted or decorated with porcupine quill designs of red and white.

Women wore their hair long and gathered at the neck, but the men fashioned theirs to suit themselves.

The largest unit of each of these tribes was the band. There were no tribal chiefs. Each band or village had its own chief. Each clan also had a chief. Tribal matters were handled by a council of chiefs. A child belonged to the clan of his father. A boy and his mother, therefore, belonged to different clans. Clan members had to marry outside of their clan.

Each of these tribes had a number of clans named after animals such as Bear or Wolf. In one case the Miami had a clan named Acorn, which was unusual as most Indians believed that a clan animal gave them supernatural power.

The women did the field work, took care of the children, did the moving, made the clothing, did the cooking, and did the weaving.

208

Sauk and Fox Indians played lacrosse with skill, strength and stamina. Sometimes there were hundreds of players on a mile-long field.

The men cleared land for the fields, made tools and weapons, engaged in warfare, did the hunting, and handled the political and religious activities.

Weapons were wooden clubs, spears, and bows and arrows. Spears and arrows had tips of chipped flint. Tools included flint knives and scrapers, bone needles and weaving tools, and stone axes. The utensils used were wooden mortars and pestles, pottery bowls, wooden bowls, mussel-shell spoons and ladles, and rawhide containers. Musical instruments included drums, rattles, flutes, whistles, and rasps.

The *Midewiwin,* or Grand Medicine Society, was an important religious organization. Members of the society were believed to be able to cure the sick and to keep the tribe successful by supernatural means. There were four ranks of members. Each had a specific degree of importance and could perform certain functions.

Chief Black Hawk of the Sauk Indians

CHEROKEE

The Cherokee of the southern Appalachians were historically and culturally one of the most important Indian peoples of the United States. Four hundred years ago when the explorer De Soto ran across the Cherokee there were about twenty-five thousand of them.

They were a powerful nation that possessed a vast hunting range. This territory included what is now northern Alabama and Georgia, western Virginia, North Carolina, South Carolina, and eastern Tennessee. Various other tribes kept them from expanding into additional territory.

The Cherokee Nation was a confederacy of towns. The total number of towns was probably fifty or more. It was hard to determine the exact number because the locations were changed quite frequently.

These Cherokee Indians hunted, fished, gardened, and collected wild plant products. Deer, rabbit, possum and turkey were available. Corn and beans were grown on a community wide basis. Herbs were collected in the hills, greens by the water, and wild grapes in the mountains. Each fall great quantities of chestnuts were collected for winter use. Corn was either saved on the ear or pounded into corn-meal. The meal would then be made into cakes and cooked in hot ashes.

When dressed the Cherokee used animal skins or cloth woven from turkey feathers sewn to strips of soft bark. The men wore a breechclout of deerskin and sometimes moccasins. Women wore a short deerskin skirt.

Tattooing was a universal practice. The face and body were also painted in preparation for games, war, and social functions.

Ancient Cherokee dwellings were circular structures of logs, poles, and bark, sometimes partially covered with earth. In some cases community buildings would be 30 feet in diameter and 20 feet high. Beds were made of cane. During the summer, meetings and social functions would be held in open pavilions.

The Cherokee believed that they were given their land by the

212

Sequoia, a Cherokee, invented an alphabet and, in one of the most remarkable achievements in Indian history, made the Cherokee literate.

"Great Spirit." They believed that the rivers were the paths to the underworld to which they would go when they died. They also believed that animals were people too.

The basis of the Cherokee moral code was what was known as the "blood law." Under this rule every death other than a natural one was punishable by death. This was on an eye-for-an-eye basis. The family of the deceased carried out the death sentence by taking the life of the murderer or one of his close relatives.

One of the most remarkable achievements in Indian history occurred in the early nineteenth century when Sequoyah, a Cherokee, invented a syllabic alphabet. The alphabet was so constructed that it could be mastered in a couple of days. The Cherokee soon became a literate people after the tribe's formal adoption of the alphabet in 1821. Type was made for each letter and in 1827 the first Indian press was established in North America. A year later printing was done in both English and Cherokee.

The Cherokee had been in the southern mountains for over two centuries before they saw their first white man. This was Hernando de Sota, who came exploring in 1540.

Other contacts with white men were made between the fifteen and seventeen hundreds. These involved some trading, exploring, and fighting. Trade in animal skins became part of the Cherokee economy. The gun became a very important addition as a weapon.

In the seventeen and eighteen hundreds the white man began pressing in from all sides. New treaties were continually made with the Cherokee. Gradually they lost their original land. Some voluntarily migrated westward. Others were forced to do so. The discovery of gold on their land made matters worse as it then became even more desirable in the eyes of the whites.

The Civil War caused more conflict as many Cherokee held slaves. Hundreds of Cherokee fought on both sides during the conflict.

Over the years many of the Cherokee married with non-Cherokee so at the present time there are few that are full-blooded. At the

214

present time about 2,000 live on a reservation in North Carolina. It is estimated that about 40,000 persons with some Cherokee blood live west of the Mississippi river at the present time.

Woodland Indian woman farming with a handmade tool

Chapter VII

THE INDIAN TODAY

THE INDIAN TRIBES mentioned in this book, along with hundreds of others, felt the impact of the white man as he moved in to what was Indian country. The white man came from the East, the North, and the South. As one Indian chief said, "The white man is as many as the sands of the sea."

Descriptions of these Indians and their way of life showed us how they lived before the white man came, when the white man arrived on the scene, and during the days of warfare between the two. The Indian's way of life could not stand up against the ever-pushing hundreds of white men with their advanced ways of living. The white man took what he wanted. When he discovered good land with Indians on it he drove them off or confined the Indians on reservations.

During the colonial period of our country, when England was in command of most of the eastern part of North America, treaties were made with the Indian tribes of the Eastern Woodlands. These tribes were treated as independent nations.

The English and others made a practice of paying a small price for the Indian lands that they wanted. Since individual Indians did not own the land, as it belonged to all of the Indians in the tribe, they did not understand what they were doing when they sold their land. In many cases they thought that they were just letting a particular group of white men use it. The Indians could not understand that white men would keep coming, and coming, and force them to leave.

As the Indians of the Eastern Woodlands were forced to sell

their land, most agreed to exchange land east of the Mississippi River for land west of the river. This meant moving Eastern Indians into the Great Plains area that was already occupied by the Plains Indians. These Eastern Indians, many of whom depended upon gardening for food, had to find new sources of food in the plains area which was buffalo country. Many took to hunting the buffalo and other wild animals.

A Bureau of Indian Affairs was created in the War Department in 1824, to manage the affairs of the Indians. When the Department of the Interior was established in 1849, the Bureau of Indian Affairs was transferred to that department. They probably moved some 70,000 Indians from the east to the west. Many promises were made to the Indians at this time. Some of these promises were kept and some were not.

During the period of time when the western states were being admitted to the Union and throughout the Civil War, Indian Tribes were still treated as nations. Since there was no place to push the Indians of the Plains and the Northwest Coast, they were placed on reservations or, in some cases, smaller tribes were just put off their land and no provision was made for them.

When the Civil War was over, soldiers and others wanted land for farms and ranches. New treaties had to be made to provide more land for the settlers. The states of the southwest came into the Union and this brought more Indians and additional Indian problems.

From the end of the Civil War to World War I, the United States Government started a program of strict Indian reservation control and tried to keep the Indians on the reservations. Indian reservations were set up on what usually turned out to be the most undesirable land from the Mississippi River to the Pacific Ocean and from the Canadian border to Mexico. For the most part, the Indians did not change their way of life but tried to live as they had in the past. To get the Indians to live like other Americans and to farm for a living, many reservations were cut up and allotted to individuals.

217

Jim Thorpe was a famous athlete, an Olympic decathlon winner

This did not work, for the Indians did not know how to use the land, and were not accustomed to handling land on an individual basis.

After World War I and during the depression that soon followed, the United States government took a new look at the Indian problem. In 1924, by an act of Congress, all Indians, no matter where they lived, were made citizens of our country. Indian groups were encouraged to reorganize. One of the major improvements under the Indian Service was the extension of schools for most of the Indian tribes.

World War II came and a large number of Indians volunteered to fight for their country. Many others were drafted. The Navaho made a particular contribution, for they were used in the signal corps because they could converse in their native language and the enemy could not understand them. Many more thousands of Indians went to work in the war industries.

Tribes and bands were encouraged to reorganize and develop towns, ranches and industry. Of 266 tribes and bands eligible for financial assistance under the Indian Reorganization Act, of 1934, 189 accepted. These then had a good start toward living and working as their fellow Americans do. The ban that had previously been placed on the use of Indian languages and Indian ceremonies was removed.

Tribes that had been dwindling started to show an increase in population. Most reservations were too small and could not be enlarged. Indians were then encouraged to leave the reservations and secure jobs on ranches and in industry. More schools were set up so that Indians could be educated for many types of work.

Because of the many disputes regarding the fairness of the settlement of the various claims of the Indians by the Federal Government, Congress passed the Indian Claims act in 1946. This gave all Indians five years to submit claims that they thought they might have against the Federal Government. This was later renewed and extended until 1962, and is being further extended by Congress beyond 1962. Approximately 852 claims were filed by various tribes, bands, and other organized groups of Indians. As these claims are settled many Indians will be awarded sums of money in payment. Other Indian claims will not be considered correct and no awards will be made in these cases.

At the present time the American Indians, including the Eskimo and Aleut number about 32,000 in Alaska, some 400,000 in the other states, and about 118,000 in Canada. Most tribes are now increasing in size. Some died out entirely during the 300 years while America was being discovered and settled. War, disease, and new living conditions caused losses in others. The American Indian of today is becoming used to a different kind of diet and housing.

Today, many Indians are solving their economic problems by taking jobs in business and industry. The larger number of Indians, however, continue to live on reservations where they farm and take seasonal work off the reservation. In general, the income for Indian families is much smaller than their non-Indian neighbors. Indians are attached to the life on the reservation and therefore hesitate to leave. The Federal Government continues its program of trying to provide jobs both on the reservations and off the reservations for all of the Indians.

The woodworking and fish-eating Indians of the Northwest, the diggers-of-roots and makers-of-baskets of California, the farmers and hunters of the Eastern Woodlands, and the buffalo hunters and raiders of the plains, that we talked about in this book, for the most part are no more. Since the white hunters, farmers, and settlers chose to take over North America for their own, it has been remade. What was once a quiet wilderness that provided the necessities of life for those who knew how to take them, has been turned into a checkerboard of organized farms, industries, businesses and homes. The Indian of today must become a part of what is known as modern civilization, he cannot go back.

220

As the Indian today becomes a part of modern civilization, he brings a rich cultural heritage with him.